SCHOLASTIC

MASTERING SCIENCE

Course Book 6

All photographs and illustrations from PhotosIndia.com Pvt. Ltd. except the ones listed below, which are from Fables.

Sugar cane (P) pg9; Cloves (P) pg 9; Parasite (P) pg12; Scavenger (P) pg12; Silkworms cocoon (P) pg29; Weaving (P) pg31; Manual threshing (P) pg48; Mechanical threshing (P) pg48; Separation of immiscible liquids (I) pg51; Thermometer (I) pg61; Plant (P) pg65; Horse (P) pg66; Elephant (P) pg70; Tap root (P) pg85; Simple leaf (P) pg87; Flower (I) pg89; Insect pollination (P) pg91; Skeleton (I) pg98; Earthworms (I) pg101; Fish (I) pg103; Snake (I) pg104; Measuring tape (P) pg115; Scale (P) pg115; LED (P) pg121; Opaque object (P) pg123; Shadow (P) pg123; Pinhole camera (I) pg125; Image (baby) (P) pg126; Water cycle (I) pg157; Rainwater harvesting (I) pg160; Bins (P) pg177; Plastic container (P) pg182

Published by Scholastic India Pvt. Ltd.

A subsidiary of Scholastic Inc., New York, 10012 (USA)

Publishers since 1920, with international operations in Canada, Australia, New Zealand, the United Kingdom, India, and Hong Kong.

For information regarding permission, write to:
Scholastic India Pvt. Ltd.
A-27, Ground Floor, Bharti Sigma Centre
Infocity-1, Sector 34, Gurgaon (Haryana) 122001, India
Email: education@scholastic.co.in

Layout, design and typesetting: Mansi Bansal
Series editor: Sonia Kapoor

First edition: 2010
Reprinted: 2011 (twice), 2012, 2013, 2014 (twice), 2015, 2016 (twice), 2017, 2018, 2019, 2023,

ISBN-13: 978-81-8477-491-7

Contents

Introduction

Mastering Science is a comprehensive series targetted at the middle school. Devised within the framework recommended by the CBSE, this series aims to spark the students' interest in science, encourage them to actively participate in the learning process, and gain a thorough understanding of scientific terms and concepts. The aim of this series is to encourage students to be curious about scientific phenomenon and explore them logically.

The main features of the series:

- It has been designed keeping in mind the thematic and activity-oriented approach recommended by the CBSE.
- Difficult-to-understand concepts and everyday scientific phenomenon are explained in a clear, concise and lucid manner.
- Colourful illustrations, numerous photographs and examples help students gain a clear understanding of the topics under discussion.
- The series complies with the **Comprehensive and Continuous Evaluation** (CCE) approach recommended by the CBSE. To make it more convenient for teachers, an evaluation sheet that provides for a thorough understanding of the student's capabilities and grasp of the lessons is provided with all books in the series.
- Amazing facts relevant to the topic under discussion are provided in every lesson in a section titled **Factastic**.
- The **Think it Over** section comprises inferential questions that encourage students to think independently. This is in tune with the Higher Order Thinking Skills (HOTS) emphasised by the CBSE.
- The **Explore** and **Learn More** sections encourage the student to gather, classify and understand

information. This reinforces the concepts within the chapter and forms a tool for independent learning for the students.

- **Circle Time** provides students a platform to share their ideas and understanding of topics with their peers.
- Every lesson is followed by a **Revision** section to help revise and reinforce concepts.
- Hands-on and easy-to-do experiments encourage analysis and reasoning, allowing the students to confidently carry out the procedure and reach a logical conclusion.
- Difficult words are explained in a glossary on the page where they appear.
- Brainteasers, puzzles and riddles, which form a part of every chapter, add a fun element to the text.

Biman Basu is the author of several popular science series and is the editor of a popular Indian science monthly. A former scientist with the prestigious Council of Scientific and Industrial Research (CSIR), Biman Basu has over thirty years of experience in writing for children. He has scripted several TV science documentaries and published more than 1,000 articles on popular science topics in various publications. He is the winner of the 'NCSTC National Award for Science Popularisation in 1994', awarded annually by the Department of Science and Technology, Government of India. He was conferred the 'AWIC Honour 2007' by the Association of Writers and Illustrators for Children for his contribution to children's literature.

1 Our Food

Uncooked food

All living beings need food to stay alive, obtain energy and to grow, but the kind of food they eat differs. The food that plants live on is different from the food that animals eat. Plants manufacture their own food using sunlight, water, carbon dioxide and nutrients from soil. Human beings eat a variety of food items, most of which need to be cooked before they can be consumed. Fruits and some vegetables can be consumed raw.

Cooked food

Explore

Make a list of the food items that can be eaten raw. Find out why some food items cannot be eaten raw. Why can't you eat a raw potato when you can eat a raw carrot? What does cooking do to food?

The food that human beings eat at different times of the day varies widely. For example, what we eat at breakfast is different from what we eat at lunch, which may be different from what we have at dinner. Sometimes, we also have snacks in between.

Circle Time

Discuss with your classmates the food items that they eat for dinner. What are the most common food items consumed in the different states of India?

Explore

On an outlined map of India, write the names of the most popular food items of each state.

Rice

Most of the foods that we eat are prepared from simple ingredients such as rice, *atta*, dal, vegetables, oil, *ghee*, sugar, salt and spices. A large variety of dishes can be made using different combinations of these ingredients and different methods of cooking or processing.

Atta

Dal

Oil

Salt

Factastic

Rice is one of the most important cereal crops. It is the staple food of over 3 billion people, which is over half of the world's population.

Spices

Boiling rice in water

Frying pakoras in oil

Cooking involves many processes. Boiling something, such as rice, in water is the simplest method of cooking. Other methods of cooking food may involve frying, roasting or baking or a combination of some of these. Roasting and frying are done at much higher temperatures than boiling. Cooking adds taste and flavour to food and makes it edible.

Roasting corn on fire

Baking a cake in an oven

cereal: grains used as food, for example, rice, wheat, maize or rye

Learn More

Watch your parents cook your favourite dish in the kitchen and make a list of the ingredients that are used and the different steps involved in the cooking process. Find out which of the methods—roasting, baking, frying or boiling—were used.

Brainteaser

Unscramble the words below to find names of food items.

1. KILM	2. GGE	3. REBDA	4. NABANAS	5. RCRASTO
6. PPAEL	7. LSTA	8. GSAUR	9. IREC	10. HATEW

Answers: 1. Milk 2. Egg 3. Bread 4. Bananas 5. Carrots 6. Apple 7. Salt 8. Sugar 9. Rice 10. Wheat

Sources of food materials

The food that we eat comes from different sources. Some food items are obtained from plants while others are animal products.

Factastic

About 2,000 species of plants are grown for consumption. Many plants have distinct cultivated varieties that are used as food.

Plant parts as food

Fruits	 Grapes Apple	Stems	 Sugar cane Onion
Flowers	 Broccoli Cauliflower	Leaves	 Lettuce
Seeds	 Wheat Kidney beans	Roots	 Carrot Turnip
		Buds	 Clove

ingredients: foods or substances combined to make a particular dish

Animal products as food

Common plant products include fruits, seeds, leaves, stem, roots, tubers, bulbs, grains, cooking oils, turmeric, sugar and a wide variety of spices. Animal products include milk, butter, ghee, cheese, curd, eggs, fish, chicken and meat. Common salt is a product extracted from sea water.

Factastic

Some foods are neither produced by plants nor by animals alone, but are produced partly by plants and partly by animals. Honey is a unique product, made by honey bees using the nectar from flowers.

Plant parts as food

Plant products used as food come from different parts of the plant. Leaves and fruits are the most commonly consumed plant parts. Roots, rhizomes, tubers, bulbs, stems, buds, flowers and seeds are also consumed.

Mustard plant

There are plants of which more than one part can be eaten. For example, the stem, flower and fruits of the banana plant are all edible. Seeds of mustard plants can be used to extract oil or used to add flavour to some dishes and its leaves are used as a vegetable (*sarson ka saag*).

Banana plant

rhizome: horizontal underground plant stems capable of producing the shoot and root systems of a new plant
tuber: short, thickened, mostly underground stem that constitutes the resting stage of certain plant seeds
bulb: a rounded underground storage component present in some plants
nectar: a sugary fluid secreted within flowers collected by bees to make honey

Learn More

Use the internet or an encyclopaedia to make a table of the food items that are obtained from plants and the plant parts they are obtained from.

Brainteaser

List the following items under the correct column in the table below.

cauliflower	wheat	milk	rice	potatoes
carrots	paneer	salt	almonds	onions
spices	radish	cheese	sugar	cream
cucumber	maize	pulses	spinach	lemon

Dairy product	Grocery	Vegetable

Growing plants from seeds

Most plants can be grown from seeds. Dry seeds can be stored for a long time. In the presence of water, ambient temperature and sunshine seeds may sprout white tips. A sprout is actually the shoot that will grow into a plant if planted in the soil. Sprouted seeds can be eaten after washing. They are high on taste and nutrition.

Sprouted seeds

Explore

Soak a handful of dry whole *moong* or *chana* seeds in two cups of water for a day. Throw the

water away from one cup and wrap the swollen seeds loosely in a piece of wet cloth. Keep it aside, taking care that the cloth does not dry up. Keep the seeds in the other cup submerged in water. Observe for one or two days. Which seeds have sprouted? Why?

Brainteaser

Several methods of cooking are used in the kitchen. Give two examples of food items that are cooked using the following methods.

Grilling	Frying	Roasting
Steaming	Baking	

Feeding habits of animals

Herbivore

Different animals eat different kinds of food. Some eat only plants. They are called **herbivores**. Some animals eat other, smaller animals. They are called **carnivores**. Some animals eat plants and other animals. They are called **omnivores**. Certain types of animals known as **scavengers**, feed on dead animals. **Parasites** are small animals that obtain their food from other animals that are alive. Mosquitoes, fleas, leeches and bugs suck the blood from other living animals for their survival. Roundworm, tapeworm, hookworm are examples of parasites that live inside the bodies of other animals.

Scavengers

Carnivore

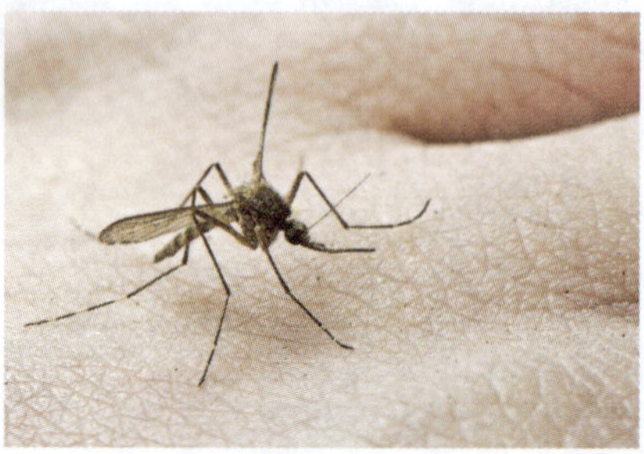

Parasite

Omnivore

Explore

Make a list of animals that you see around your home and find out what they eat. Visit a zoo and find out the kind of food consumed by the animals. Group the animals into three categories: herbivores, carnivores and omnivores.

Revision Time

- ✶ There is a wide variety of food that we eat at different times of the day.
- ✶ A wide variety of food is eaten in the different states of India.
- ✶ The main sources of food are plants and animals.
- ✶ Plant products that we use as food come from different parts of plants.
- ✶ Herbivores are animals that eat only plants.
- ✶ Carnivores are animals that eat other animals.
- ✶ Omnivores are animals that eat both plants as well as other animals.

Quiz Time

1. Answer the questions.

a. What are the main sources of food?

b. What does cooking do to food?

c. Why is honey a unique food?

d. What are plant-eating animals known as?

e. How do parasites obtain their food?

2. Fill in the blanks.

a. Rice can be cooked by ____________________.

b. Cinnamon is obtained from the ____________________ of the cinnamon tree.

c. Frying is done at a ____________________ temperature than boiling.

d. Carnivores eat only ____________________.

e. Milk, curd, butter, ghee are all ____________________ products.

3. Indicate whether the statements are true or false.

a. Common salt is extracted from plants. True False

b. Sugar is a plant product. True False

c. Ginger is the root of the ginger plant. True False

d. Bread is made by frying. True False

e. Sugar cane is a kind of grass. True False

4. Explain the terms.

a. sprouting

b. roasting

c. pickling

d. frying

e. marinating

5. Project Work

a. In the table below, the left-hand column shows a list of animals. Use an encyclopaedia or the internet to find out what these animals eat.

Name of animals	Food they eat
buffalo	
tiger	
horse	
cat	
dog	
cow	
whale	
lizard	
crow	
spider	
camel	
cobra	

b. Classify the animals given in the previous table as herbivores, carnivores or omnivores.

Herbivores	Carnivores	Omnivores

Think it over

1. The contents of a raw egg—the yellow yolk and the colourless albumen—are liquids. Boiling an egg turns them into solids. Why?
2. If milk is kept at room temperature without boiling for a long time, it turns sour and gets spoiled. But boiling milk frequently prevents it from getting spoilt. What happens on boiling?

2 Components of Food

Food is made up of many different components. A meal may consist of rice, dal, fish curry, some vegetables and yoghurt, or it may be chapati with vegetables, or a combination of rice, *sambar*, *avial* and buttermilk. The main component of most meals is some item made of starch, which is a **carbohydrate**. A balanced meal also includes **proteins**, **fats**, **fibres** and **water**.

Explore

Find out from your friends what they ate in the morning. Look up an encyclopaedia or the internet to find out what each food item they ate may contain. Make a table classifying carbohydrates, proteins, fats and fibres.

We get food ingredients from plant or animal sources. The various components of a meal provide energy to our body. These are called nutrients. Apart from starch, proteins and fats, our body also needs vitamins, minerals and dietary fibres. It is possible to find out if a particular food item (both raw and cooked) contains starch, protein or fat by simple chemical tests that can be carried out in the school laboratory.

Activity

Aim: Demonstrate the presence of starch, protein and fat.

Material required: iodine solution, test tubes, potato, milk/eggs, potato chips or butter, copper sulphate solution, caustic soda solution, piece of paper

Method: Divide the class into three groups. Each group perfoms one task.

nutrients: substances that provide nourishment essential for the maintenance and growth of the body.
dietary fibre: the indigestible portion of plant foods that pushes food through the digestive system, absorbs water and eases bowel movement

Group 1

To test for the presence of starch in a food item, take a small amount of the food item, for example potato, in a test tube

and add a few drops of iodine solution to it. If starch is present in the food item, the colour of the iodine solution will change to blue-black.

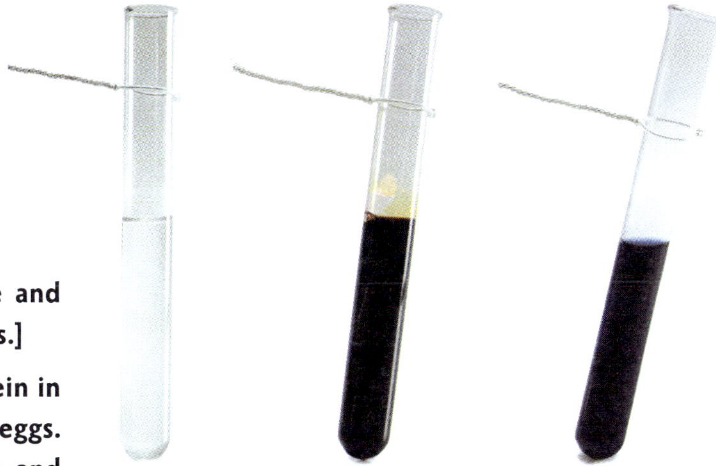

Water   Iodine solution   Presence of starch

Group II

[Caution: Both copper sulphate and caustic soda are highly poisonous.]

To test for the presence of protein in a food item, for example milk or eggs. Powder or mash the food item and place a small amount of it in a test tube. Add ten drops of water, shake well and then add two drops of copper sulphate solution and ten drops of caustic soda solution to it. Shake well and allow the test tube to stand for a few minutes. The colour of the solution will turn violet if protein is present.

Group III

To test for the presence of fat in a food item, for example potato chips, wrap the piece of food to be tested in a piece of dry paper and crush it. After unwrapping, spread the paper flat and let it dry for some time to remove any water. Look for any oily patches that seem bright when held up against light. An oily patch shows the presence of fat.

Brainteaser

Unscramble the following words to form the names of the food groups.

1. TAFS
2. MVINSATI
3. TPSORNEI
4. NLSAREIM
5. RFSEBI
6. DCYHORABSTAER

Answers: 1. fats 2. vitamins 3. proteins 4. minerals 5. fibres 6. carbohydrates

Role of nutrients

Each of the different types of food classes—carbohydrates, fats, proteins, vitamins, minerals and fibres—are essential for the proper growth and development of the body. Carbohydrates, such as rice, *atta* and sugar, are the main sources of energy.

Carbohydrates

Fats give us energy. In fact, compared to the same amount of carbohydrates, fats give much more energy. Fats play an important role in maintaining healthy skin and hair, insulating body organs against shock, maintaining body temperature and promoting healthy cell function.

Fats

Factastic

Starch is the most important carbohydrate in the human diet and is present in many staple foods. The major sources of starch are rice, wheat, maize, potatoes and cassava. Widely used foods items containing starch are bread, pancakes, cereals, noodles, pasta, porridge and tortilla.

Proteins are needed for the growth and repair of the body. Proteins build, maintain and replace the tissues in our body. The muscles, organs and the immune system are made up mostly of protein. Several food items contain protein, but the best sources are meat, poultry, fish, eggs, dairy products, nuts, seeds and legumes such as black beans and dals.

Vitamins are of many kinds and are known by different names. Some of these are vitamin A, vitamin C, vitamin D, vitamin E and vitamin K. There is also a group of vitamins called

Proteins

tissue: part of an organism made up of cells having a similar structure and function
immune system: the organs and processes of the body that protect us from infection

vitamin B-complex. The body needs all types of vitamins in small quantities for proper growth and to maintain good health. Vitamins help protecting the body against diseases and keep our eyes, bones, teeth and gums healthy. The deficiency of certain vitamins could lead to diseases.

Explore

Use an encyclopaedia or the internet to find out how the different vitamins help us in maintaining good health and what happens if we take too little of any of them.

Minerals, such as iron, calcium and iodine, are needed by the body in very minute amounts. However, if they are not included in the diet, it may lead to many health problems. Macrominerals are needed in large quantities while trace minerals are needed in very small amounts by the body. Examples of macrominerals are calcium, magnesium, potassium and sodium while zinc, copper, iron and iodine are examples of trace minerals.

Circle Time

Discuss with your friends whether you would remain healthy if you consumed only dairy products and nothing else. Give reasons for your answer.

Explore

Make a chart with drawings or photos of various food items indicating the minerals and vitamins they contain.

Brainteaser

We all know that junk food is unhealthy. However, we can alter the way some of these junk food items are prepared in order to turn them into healthy food items. For example, we can make a pizza healthy by using a base made of whole wheat and topping it with a lot of vegetables.

How can the following food items be made healthy?

1. samosa
2. noodles
3. chips
4. fries
5. burger

deficiency: a lack or shortage

Besides carbohydrates, proteins, fats, minerals and vitamins, the body also needs **dietary fibre** and water. Dietary fibre is also known as roughage, which is the indigestible portion of plant food. Whole grains and pulses, potatoes, fresh fruits and vegetables are the main sources of roughage. Roughage does not provide any nutrient to the body, but adds to the bulk of food. This helps the body get rid of undigested food and keep the bowel movements normal.

Factastic
Seventy per cent of the human body consists of water. Ninety per cent of blood and 85 per cent of our brain is water.

Water is essential for life. When taken with food it helps the body to absorb nutrients from food. It also helps in getting rid of some wastes from the body in the form of urine and sweat. We get most of the water that the body needs from the liquids we drink such as water, juices, milk and soup. In addition, we also get water from fruits, vegetables and many cooked foods.

Sources of nutrients

carbohydrates (sugar and starch)	sugar: sugar cane, fruits, honey, chocolates, sweets, milk starch: rice, wheat, bread, potatoes, maize, corn
proteins	milk and dairy products, pulses such as *moong* dal, fish, meat, eggs, soya beans
fats	peanuts, ghee, oil, almonds and other dry fruits, butter, meat, fish, eggs, milk, cheese
vitamins	fruits, vegetables, fish
minerals	green leafy vegetables, dairy products, citrus fruits, beans, peanuts, fish, pulses, eggs
dietary fibre or roughage	carrot, cabbage, strawberry, peach

Deficiency diseases

Merely consuming enough food may not lead to good health. If food lacking in a nutrient is taken over a long period of time, the person may suffer from the deficiency of that particular nutrient. Deficiency of one or more nutrients may cause diseases or health disorders. Diseases that occur due to the lack of nutrients are called **deficiency diseases**.

For example, the deficiency of protein in food over a long period may lead to stunted growth, swelling of the face, discolouration of the hair, skin diseases or diarrhoea. If the diet is deficient in both carbohydrates and proteins, it may affect body growth. Such a person becomes so weak that he/she may not even be able to move.

The deficiency of different vitamins and minerals may also result in certain diseases or disorders. For example, the deficiency of iron, which is essential for the formation of red blood cells, may cause anaemia, a condition leading to weakness. The deficiency of calcium leads to weak bones.

All deficiency diseases can be prevented by having a balanced diet. A balanced diet consists of the right combination of carbohydrates, proteins, fats and vitamins. A complete meal should also contain sufficient amounts of roughage and water. Taking too much or too little of any one of these is bad for health.

Explore

Find out from an encyclopaedia or the internet what is the right combination of carbohydrates, proteins, fats, vitamins and minerals in a balanced diet. Make a food chart for yourself and then check if you eat a balanced diet.

Cooking food

Most fruits and some vegetables, such as carrot, radish, onion, turnip and lettuce, can be eaten raw because our body can digest them. But grains, such as rice, wheat or maize, as well as vegetables, such as potato, brinjal, pumpkin and drumsticks, and *urad* or *masoor* dal cannot be eaten raw because they cannot be digested. Cooking makes food soft, tasty and easily digestible. But over-cooking destroys some nutrients and vitamins such as vitamin C and others. After boiling vegetables, the cooking water should not be thrown away, since it contains soluble proteins and minerals from the boiled vegetables.

Food grains

Crops, such as rice and wheat, are grown in fields. Rice and wheat are actually seeds. While they are developing, the seeds are covered with a thin protective layer, which on drying becomes the husk. The husk cannot be eaten. As the crop ripens, the plants are cut and the grains separated by threshing. The separated grains are then dehusked.

Mechanised threshing process

Winnowing

The dehusked grains are separated from the chaff by a process known as winnowing where wind is used to blow away the chaff. The dehusked and cleaned grains are then sent to the market for sale.

Revision Time

- Food is made up of many different components.
- The main component of most meals is starch, which is a carbohydrate.
- A balanced diet includes carbohydrates, proteins, fats, fibres, vitamins, minerals, water and roughage.
- Carbohydrates and fats are the main sources of energy for the body.
- Proteins are needed for the growth and repair of the body.
- Vitamins help in protecting the body against diseases and in keeping the eyes, bones, teeth and gums healthy.
- Minerals are needed by the body in very minute amounts, their deficiency may result in many health problems.
- Dietary fibre and water are important components of a complete and balanced meal.
- The lack of one or more nutrients in the body over a long period may result in deficiency diseases.

Quiz Time

1. Answer the questions.

a. What are the main components of our food?

b. How are carbohydrates useful for the body?

c. Why is iron needed in our diet?

d. Which food items provide roughage in our diet?

e. What is a balanced diet?

2. Fill in the blanks.

a. ____________________ in our diet helps build muscles and repair tissues in our body.

b. Deficiency of iron in diet causes ____________________.

c. The presence of starch in food can be tested by using ____________________.

d. Fruits, such as lemon, orange and guava, contain vitamin ____________________.

e. Minerals are required in ____________________ amounts.

3. Explain the terms.

a. anaemia

b. roughage

c. carbohydrate

d. proteins

e. deficiency diseases

4. Indicate whether the statements are true or false.

a.	Carbohydrates help in building muscles.	True	False
b.	Rice is a good source of protein.	True	False
c.	Calcium deficiency leads to weak bones.	True	False
d.	Milk is a rich source of calcium.	True	False
e.	Vitamin A is necessary for good eyesight.	True	False

5. Project Work

a. In the table below, the first column shows a list of food items. Use an encyclopaedia or the internet to find out what vitamins and minerals these items contain and complete the table.

Food item	Vitamins	Minerals
milk		
eggs		
butter		
apple		
orange		
spinach		
carrot		
liver		
fish		
almond		

b. In the table below, the first column has a list of food items. The other three columns are the three main components of food. Tick [✔] the correct column if the nutrient is present in the food item.

Food item	Carbohydrate	Protein	Fat
rice			
fish			
meat			
wheat			
milk			
egg			
apple			
corn flakes			
sugar			
moong dal			

c. In the table below, the first column gives a list of vitamins and minerals essential for good health. Use an encyclopaedia or the internet to find out the diseases and their symptoms caused by the deficiency of these vitamins and minerals.

Vitamin/Mineral	Deficiency disease/disorder	Symptoms
vitamin A		
vitamin B1		
vitamin C		
vitamin D		
vitamin E		
iron		
calcium		
iodine		

Think it over

1. **Frying finger chips takes much less time than cooking a potato by boiling it. Why?**
2. **Why does cutting an onion bring tears to your eyes but cutting an onion in a bowl of water does not?**

3 Clothes

Cotton shirt

Clothes come in a wide range of types and colours and are made from a variety of materials called fabrics. Fabrics are produced by weaving or knitting textile fibres, which can be natural or made artificially (synthetics). In the past, all fabrics were made from natural fibres obtained from plant and animal sources. However, in the twentieth century, these were supplemented by artificial fibres made from petroleum. Some fabrics, such as cotton, keep us cool in summer, while others, such as woollens, keep us warm in winter. Apart from clothing, fabrics are also used for other household purposes. They are used to make bedsheets, blankets, curtains, tablecloths, towels, mattresses, dusters, gunny bags and even schoolbags.

Woollen sweater

Source of fabrics

All fabrics are made by weaving or knitting yarn or thread of different kinds. Yarn in turn is made by spinning even thinner strands called fibres—natural or synthetic. Spinning twists the fibres, making them stay together hence giving strength to the yarn.

Weaving loom with cloth being made on it

fabric: cloth made by weaving or knitting natural or synthetic fibres

Spinning of fibres to produce yarn

Explore

Tear a piece of cotton fabric and look for loose thread or yarn at the edge. Pull out the thread. Look closely under a magnifying glass. What do you find? Unravel the yarn with your fingers. How many strands do you find? What happens when you try to unravel the individual strands? Do you get an idea of how fabrics are made?

Types of fibres

Fibres are obtained from many sources. One of the most common source is cotton. Cotton is obtained from the fruits of the cotton plant (known as cotton bolls) after separating the seeds. Jute is obtained from the bark of the jute plant. Silk is obtained from the cocoon of silkworms, while wool is obtained from the fleece of sheep or goat. Cotton, jute, silk and wool are all **natural fibres**. Nylon, polyester and acrylic are artificially made in factories from chemicals obtained from petroleum. They are known as **synthetic fibres**, or simply, synthetics.

Factastic

The discovery of dyed flax fibres in a cave in the Republic of Georgia dated to 34,000BC suggests that textile-like materials were made even in prehistoric times.

Common plant fibres

Cotton

Cotton is a soft white fibre that grows around the seeds of the cotton plant in a form known as a boll. Cotton plants grow in places with black soil and warm climate, especially in the tropical and subtropical regions around the world, including India, Africa and America.

flax: textile fibre made from the stalks of the linseed plant

Cotton bolls

Factastic
Cotton was first cultivated 7,000 years ago by the inhabitants of the Indus Valley Civilisation. Today, India is the second-largest producer of cotton in the world, after China.

A single cotton plant usually bears up to 100 bolls. After maturing, the bolls burst open and the seeds covered with cotton fibres can be seen. Cotton is picked by hand or using machines. After picking, the fibres are separated from the seeds by a process called ginning. Traditionally, ginning was done manually, but nowadays machines are used for this purpose. After ginning, cotton is packed into tight bundles called bales for transportation and trade.

Jute

Jute is a long, soft, shiny, golden-coloured vegetable fibre that can be spun into coarse, strong threads. It is produced from jute plants that grow during the hot and rainy seasons. Jute is one of the cheapest natural fibres and is second only to cotton in terms of the amount produced and variety of its uses. In India, jute is mainly grown in West Bengal, Bihar and Assam.

Factastic
Jute is a very durable material and has the life span of over a thousand plastic carrier bags.

Jute fibres

Jute fibre is obtained from the thin bark of the jute plant. The cut stems of the plant are kept immersed in water for weeks after which the softened bark comes off the stalk easily. The soft bark is further loosened by beating it under

Factastic
Several historical documents, including the *Ain-e-Akbari* written by Abul Fazal in 1590, state that the poor villagers of India used to wear clothes made of jute.

Fabric made from jute

water. The fibres thus obtained are then washed, dried and packed into bales for transportation and trade.

Factastic
Jute is completely biodegradable. When it is discarded, it decomposes and puts valuable nutrients back into the soil.

Common animal fibres

Silk

Silk is a natural fibre with high lustre, obtained from cocoons made by the larvae of the mulberry silkworm, *Bombyx mori*. For the production of silk, silkworms are reared in captivity, a practice known as **sericulture**. There are several types of silk, such as *muga* and *tasar*, produced by various species of silkworms, but they are not as soft and lustrous as mulberry silk. The silk filament is drawn off the cocoons after placing them in boiling water to kill the caterpillars within. India is the second largest producer of silk in the world after China.

Silkworm cocoon

Factastic
As much as 1.5 km of silk filament can be drawn from a single cocoon of a silkworm.

Wool

Wool is a special kind of animal hair and is mainly obtained from sheep, goats, rabbits, yaks and camels. The hair of sheep has many unique properties that make it well suited for textile production. Wool is used in a variety of textiles and can be woven or knitted. Wool is obtained by a process known as shearing, which involves cutting the hair of the animal. It is usually done once a year. After shearing, the wool is washed to remove fatty impurities and then it is dyed and then spun into yarn.

shearing: removing by cutting off or clipping

Wool being obtained from a sheep by shearing

Circle Time

Collect small pieces of fabrics made of cotton, jute, silk and wool. Hold the tip of each piece over a flame. When it starts burning remove it from the flame and notice how the smoke smells. Do you notice the difference between the burning smells of different fabrics? What do they tell you about their composition? Discuss with your friends.

Factastic

Wool is stronger than steel and is water-, wrinkle- and fire resistant.

Spinning yarn

The process of making yarn from fibres is called spinning. In this process, fibres from cotton wool or other sources are drawn out and twisted. This brings the fibres together to form a yarn. A simple device used for spinning is a hand spindle, also called a *takli*. Another hand-operated device used for spinning is the *charkha* or spinning wheel. Spinning of yarn on a large scale is done with the help of spinning machines. The spun yarn is stronger than single fibres. After spinning, yarns are used for making fabrics by weaving or knitting.

Takli or hand spindle

Explore

Try spinning cotton yarn with your fingers. Hold some cotton wool in one hand. Pinch some cotton between the thumb and forefinger of your other hand. Now, gently start pulling out the cotton, while continuously twisting the fibres with your fingers. What do you get? Does it look like thread? When spun with a spindle, it is possible to get yarn of more uniform thickness.

Making fabric

Weaving

Yarn can be converted into fabric or cloth by weaving. Weaving is the process of making cloth, blankets and other products by crossing two or more sets of threads over and under each other. Weavers use threads spun from both natural fibres such as cotton, silk and wool as well as synthetic fibres such as nylon and polyester. Weaving of cloth is usually done in looms, which are either hand-operated or power-operated. The fabric is formed in the loom by interlacing long threads passing in one direction with others at a right angle to them. The woven cloth can be plain (in one colour or a simple pattern), or it can be woven in decorative or artistic designs.

Weaving

Explore

Thin, narrow strips of almost any flexible material can be woven. People learned to weave thousands of years ago using natural grasses, leafstalks, palm leaves and thin strips of wood. You can weave a paper mat with strips of paper.

Take two sheets of thick paper of different colours, each being about 30 cm square. Draw lines on the two sheets 1-cm-wide and cut into strips. Weave the cut strips by passing them alternately above and below each other. When finished, stick the free ends of the strips with gum. You've woven a paper mat with a chequerboard design.

Knitting

Sweater being hand knitted

Knitting is a method by which a single thread or yarn may be turned into a piece of fabric. It consists of loops, called stitches, pulled through each other. Knitting is usually done by hand using knitting needles. Knitting can also be done using machines.

The method of weaving involves threads that are always straight, running parallel either lengthwise or crosswise. However, in contrast to that, the yarn in knitted fabrics follows a winding path, forming symmetric loops. Since the entire fabric may be knitted from a single thread, it is possible to undo the entire knitted fabric by pulling out the yarn from a loose end.

loom: a machine for weaving yarn into a fabric

Brainteaser

Three types of fabric weaves are shown below. Can you name them?

a.

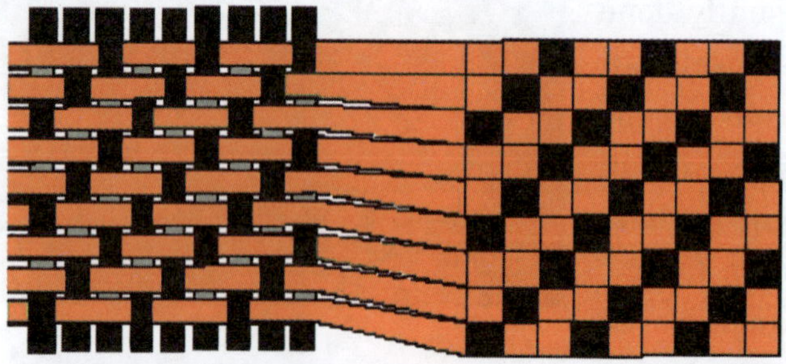

b.

c.

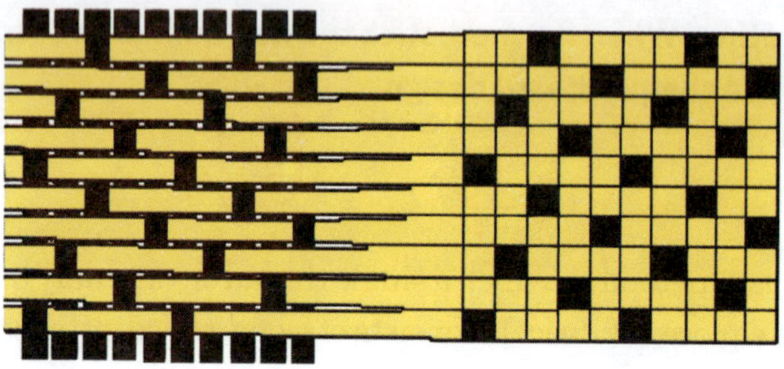

Answers: a. twill weave b. plain weave c. satin weave

The quality of a woven or knitted fabric depends on the type of yarn used, as well as on the pattern of the weave or knit. Cotton yarn can be woven into simple *khadi* or expensive gabardine. Similarly, woollen yarn can be woven into expensive suiting or knitted into a simple sweater.

Factastic

The oldest woven cloth discovered so far is a linen fabric, woven from locally grown flax. It dates back to about 7000BC and comes from a place called Cayonu in Turkey.

Clothing through the ages

Clothing made of leather

Throughout history, many materials have been used to make clothes. Materials have ranged from leather and furs to woven and knitted materials, to exotic natural and synthetic fabrics. According to archaeologists and anthropologists, possibly the earliest clothing consisted of fur, leather, leaves or grass, which were draped, wrapped or tied around the body. After people began to settle in agricultural communities, they learnt to twist animal fleece or hair together into long strands. These were woven into fabrics to be draped around the body, as stitching was not known. Early sewing needles made of bone and ivory, dating to about 30,000BC, have been found near Kostenki in Russia. But even today, when stitched clothes are widely available, un-stitched pieces of fabric, such as *sarees*, *dhotis*, *lungis* or turbans, continue to be used widely in India.

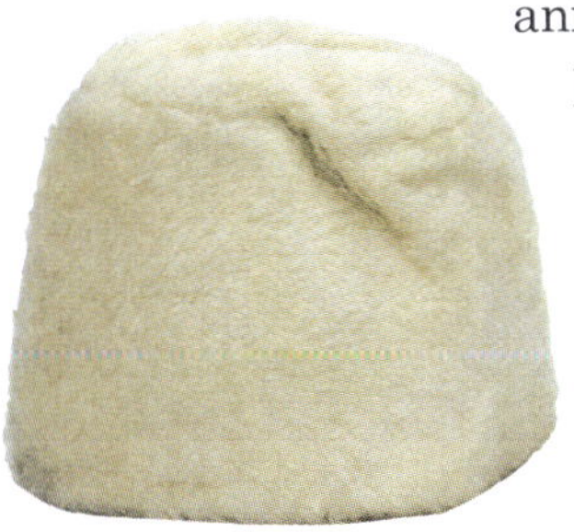

Cap made of fur

Revision Time

- Clothes come in a wide range of styles and colours and are made from a wide variety of materials called fabrics .
- In the past, all fabrics were made from natural fibres obtained from plant and animal sources.
- In the twentieth century, natural fibres were supplemented by artificial fibres made from petroleum.
- Cotton and jute are common plant fibres while silk and wool are obtained from animals.
- Yarn is made from fibres by spinning.
- All fabrics are made by weaving or knitting yarn or thread of different kinds.
- Weaving is the process of making fabrics by crossing two sets of threads over and under each other.
- Knitting is a method by which a single thread or yarn may be turned into a piece of fabric.

archaeologist: a scientist who studies prehistoric people and their culture
anthropologist: a scientist who studies human beings and their ancestors through time and space
ivory: a hard, smooth substance that makes up most of the tusks of elephants

Quiz Time

1. Answer the questions.

a. What is the climate needed to grow cotton?

b. From which animal is silk obtained?

c. By what process are cotton fibres separated from cotton seeds?

d. *Muga* and *tasar* are varieties of which fibre?

e. What is wool?

2. Fill in the blanks.

a. Cotton is a fibre obtained from ________________.

b. Yarn is made from fibre by ________________.

c. Cotton yarn can be ________________ into *khadi* cloth.

d. ________________ is a method by which a single yarn may be turned into a piece of fabric.

e. Jute is produced from the ________________ of the jute plant.

3. Explain the terms.

a. cotton bolls

b. cocoon

c. sericulture

d. caterpillar

e. interlacing

4. Indicate whether the statements are true or false.

a.	Nylon absorbs water better than cotton.	True	False
b.	In woven fabrics, threads are always straight, running parallel either lengthwise or crosswise.	True	False
c.	Yarn can be turned into fabric, or cloth, by spinning.	True	False
d.	Wool is a very good conductor of heat.	True	False
e.	Cotton is highly inflammable.	True	False

5. Project Work

a. Tick [✔] the correct column for items listed in the first column.

Item/Fabric	Plant	Animal	Synthetic	Mixed
shirt/cotton				
sari/silk				
pullover/wool				
shopping bag/jute				
towel/cotton				
socks/nylon				
curtain/cotton-silk				

b. Conduct the following tests in your school lab. You should wear rubber gloves when you perform these tests.

Take three small pieces of six different fabrics: cotton, silk, wool, jute, nylon and polyester.

Place the pieces on a ceramic tile. Put one drop of concentrated sulphuric acid (Conc. H_2SO_4), one drop of concentrated nitric acid (Conc. HNO_3) and one drop of caustic soda solution on three separate pieces of each kind of fabric. Observe what happens and record your observations in the table.

Fabric	Effect of		
	Conc. H_2SO_4	Conc. HNO_3	Caustic soda
cotton			
wool			
jute			
silk			
nylon			
polyester			

Which fabric is the most resistant to acids and alkalis?

c. Place a few drops of water on a ceramic tile. Take small pieces of different fabrics and place each piece turn by turn on the water drops. Do all the fabrics soak up the water equally well?

Think it over

1. **How do woollen garments keep us warm in winter?**
2. **Can a towel made of nylon be as good as a cotton towel?**

4 Things Around Us

We see hundreds of objects at home, in school and all around us. All these objects can be grouped into different categories based on their properties. They may be grouped according to their physical state—solid, liquid or gas. They may be grouped according to their shape—spherical, cylindrical, box-like, flat and so on. They may also be grouped on the basis of the material they are made from—such as glass, clay, metal, plastic, wood, paper, cloth, rubber and so on. In addition, there are objects that may be made up of materials belonging to more than one category.

Circle Time

Make a list in class of at least 100 different objects that you see in daily life. Make three teams. One team may divide the objects in the list based on their physical state; the second team may categorise the objects on the basis of their shape; and the third team may group the objects according to the material they are made of. Each team should present their findings in a table to the rest of the class.

Properties of materials

Baked clay *matka*

Glass jug

Materials from which objects are made differ widely in their properties. For example, a baked clay *matka* and a glass jug are both brittle and can be used to keep water. Both will break easily if dropped. But the *matka* is porous; that is, water can seep through the walls making its outside wet, while water cannot seep through the walls of a glass jug. Similarly, the metal handle of a cooking pot heats up easily, but a wooden or plastic handle does not. A screwdriver always has a plastic handle—never a metal one—because electric current can easily pass through metal but not through plastic, which is a good insulator. Thus, the material chosen to make an object depends on its properties and the purpose for which the object is to be used.

Pan with a plastic handle

Appearance

Lustre

Non-lustrous material

Materials differ widely in their appearance. The surface of unpolished wood, brick, paper and cotton or jute cloth appears rough, but the surface of most metals appears shiny. Metals usually lose lustre and appear dull if kept exposed to the air and moisture for a long time, but the freshly cut surface of a metal will always be shiny. The lustre of a dull metal object becomes visible if rubbed with fine sandpaper. Metals, such as gold and platinum, do not get tarnished when exposed to air, hence they never lose their lustre. That is why these metals are used for making jewellery. Metals, such as nickel and chromium, also do not get tarnished easily, hence these metals are used for coating copper, brass and iron objects to keep them shining and attractive.

Lustrous material

lustre: the visual property of something that shines with reflected light
tarnish: discolouration of metal surface caused by exposure to oxygen

Transparency

Glass, clear plastic, water and air are all transparent materials; they allow light to pass through making it possible to see through them. Window glass is transparent and lets the light come in, allowing people inside to have a view of the outside. All spectacle lenses are made of transparent material so that the wearer can see through them. Transparent glass or plastic containers make the contents inside clearly visible as do glass panes of display cabinets. Transparent polythene sheets are used by horticulturists to cover greenhouses.

Transparent material

Factastic

A transparent material allows light of all wavelengths to pass through with equal ease. Good sunglasses allow visible light to pass through but totally cut off ultraviolet rays that are harmful to the eye.

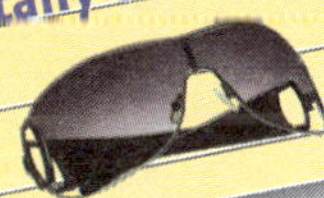

Greenhouse

In contrast to transparent materials, **opaque** materials block all light falling on them, not allowing any light to pass through. Thus a tree blocks the sunlight and a shadow appears on the other side.

It is not possible to see through opaque materials. Brick, concrete, wood, cardboard, metal sheets, cement and asbestos sheets are all opaque. Hence, objects kept inside a metal or wooden box cannot be seen from outside.

Opaque material

greenhouse: an enclosure with transparent walls and roof warmed by the sun, used for the cultivation of plants
bone china: fine translucent porcelain that contains bone ash

Some materials are neither totally transparent nor totally opaque. They are called **translucent**. Fibreglass roofs, frosted glass and fine bone china are all translucent

Fibreglass

materials. They allow some light to pass through but do not allow a clear view of objects on the other side. Factories often have roofs made of corrugated fibreglass sheets that allow the light of the sun to filter through. This helps in cutting down the costs of lighting spaces.

Frosted glass

Hardness

Diamond

Solid materials can be hard or soft. The hardness differs between materials, which gives an idea of how firm or rigid an object is and how easily it can be bent or scratched. Glass is a hard material but not as hard as diamond. Glass cannot scratch diamond so glass is softer than diamond. A piece of wood can scratch a candle. So wood is harder than candle wax. But wood can be scratched by an iron nail. So iron is harder than wood.

A nail is harder than a brick which is harder than a candle

On the other hand, materials, such as wax, rubber, plasticine and putty, are all soft materials. They can be easily compressed by pressing and can be given different shapes.

Soft material—rubber and plasticine

corrugated: shaped into alternating parallel grooves and ridges

Explore

Take a pair of steel scissors with pointed tips. Collect various objects made of different materials such as steel, aluminium, brass, plastic, glass, baked clay, porcelain, wood and wax. Using the pointed tip of the scissors, try to make a small scratch on the surface of each object. Record your observations in a table showing which materials could be scratched by the scissors.

Repeat the activity using a piece of broken glass and a piece of hard plastic.

Density

Solid objects made of different materials behave differently when placed in water. Some sink while others float. Iron nails, stone, coins, sand, crockery pieces and metal spoons sink if put in water. But objects, such as candles, corks, thermocol balls and dry leaves, float on the surface. Objects, that sink have more density than water and objects that float have less density than water.

Thermocol balls float in water

Density is defined as the mass per unit volume of a substance.

A nail, stone and coin sink in water

Explore

Take two glass tumblers. Fill each one of them about two-thirds with water. In one glass, keep adding salt and stirring till no more salt dissolves.

Take two fresh eggs and drop one in each glass. What happens? Can you explain why the eggs behave differently in the two glasses?

Oil floats on the surface of water

Liquids also behave in a similar way. Mercury sinks in water because it is denser than water but oil floats because it is less dense than water. This property of liquids comes in handy in some extraction processes.

Mercury sinks in water

Activity

Aim: Make your own hydrometer, an instrument used to measure the density of liquids.

Material required: a drinking straw, modelling clay, marker pen, salt, ruler and a glass of water

Method: Take a small ball of modelling clay and seal one end of the straw.

Put this straw with the sealed side down in a glass filled with water. Mark the straw at the point where the surface of water touches it.

Remove the straw from the glass. In the same water, add about 30 gm of salt and mix to dissolve it.

Again put the same straw in salt water and mark the point where the surface of water touches the straw.

You can add more salt and check again.

As you keep adding salt to the water, the density of water increases. What happens to the straw. Does it float in water as the density of water increases or does it sink?

Conclusion: Objects float in water if they are lighter than water or their density is less than water. Objects sink if their density is more than water.

Brainteaser

Tick the items that will float in water.

1. slice of bread ____________
2. oil ____________
3. sugar crystals ____________
4. honey ____________
5. potato chips ____________
6. a grain of rice ____________

Solubility

Many solid substances dissolve in water, while others do not. Substances such as sugar, salt and baking soda, when added to water, completely disappear after stirring. These are soluble in water and dissolve to form a solution. Water

solubility: the property of a particular substance that can dissolve in a particular solvent

Factastic

Water plays an important role in the functioning of our body because it can dissolve a large number of substances that our food produces after digestion. The dissolved substances are carried to the various parts of the body by blood.

in which sugar is dissolved tastes sweet, while water with dissolved salt tastes salty. Sea water is salty because it contains dissolved salt. The solubility of a substance can be increased by increasing the temperature of water. Substances dissolved in water can be extracted from the solution only by removing the water by boiling it.

If substances, such as sand, pebbles, chalk powder and sawdust, are put in water, they remain visible even after they have been stirred in the water for a long time. These substances are insoluble and do not dissolve in water. Insoluble substances can be easily separated from water by filtering.

Explore

Make a mixture of chalk powder, iron filings and salt. How would you separate the three components of the mixture?

Some liquids disappear when they are mixed with water because they form a solution. Alcohol, vinegar, glycerine and most inorganic acids dissolve in water and form solutions.

Some other liquids, however, such as kerosene, cooking oil, petrol and most organic liquids are insoluble in water. They do not dissolve in water. When mixed and stirred with water and kept aside for some time, they form a separate layer.

Fizz in aerated soft drinks

Explore

Take about 10 ml of tincture of iodine in a conical flask and dilute it with 50 ml of water. You'll get a yellow solution. Now add 5 ml of carbon tetrachloride to the solution with a dropper. Shake well and allow the mixture to stand.

What happens to the colour of the water layer? Where did the iodine go? Can you think of a useful application of this method?

inorganic acids: relating or belonging to the class of compounds not having a carbon basis such as hydrochloric and sulphuric acids
organic liquid: substance whose molecules contain one or more carbon atoms

Water can also dissolve some gases. Water normally contains dissolved oxygen, which makes it possible for fish and other animals that live under water to survive. Aerated soft drinks have carbon dioxide dissolved in them which makes them 'fizzy'. When sulphur dioxide and nitrogen oxide emitted from factories dissolve in raindrops, they produce acid rain, which damages stone sculptures and trees.

Activity

Aim: Make your own fizzy cocktail.

Material required: a glass filled 3/4th with water, a few drops of a food colour of your choice, two teaspoons of lemon juice, two teaspoons of sugar, two teaspoons of soda bicarbonate

Method: Add food colour to the glass of water. Mix in the sugar and stir till it dissolves. Add lemon juice and stir. Finally, add the soda bicarbonate and watch the fizz develop.

Conclusion: The acidic lemon juice and the alkaline soda bicarbonate react to form carbon dioxide (CO_2) that forms the fizz.

Revision Time

- Objects around us are made up of a large variety of materials.
- Different types of materials have different properties.
- Materials can be grouped on the basis of similarities or differences in their properties.
- Grouping materials into different categories makes it convenient to study their properties and also to observe any patterns in these properties.
- Materials differ in their appearance and the manner in which they mix in water or other liquids.
- Objects may be hard or soft; transparent, opaque or translucent; or lustrous or dull.
- Some materials float in water while others sink.
- Some materials dissolve easily in water while others do not.

Quiz Time

1. Answer the questions.

a. Why does the wooden handle of a cooking pan remain cool during cooking?

b. Why is glass used in the making of spectacle lenses?

c. Why does a tree cast a shadow on a bright sunny day?

d. Why is diamond used to cut glass?

e. By what method can an insoluble material be separated from a mixture with water?

2. Fill in the blanks.

a. Metals usually lose ________________ and appear dull if kept exposed to air and moisture for a long time.

b. ________________ materials allow some light to pass through but do not allow a clear view of objects on the other side.

c. Ice floats on water because it ________________ on freezing.

d. Water contains ________________ oxygen that supports life under water.

e. More sugar can be dissolved in water at ________________ temperatures.

3. Explain the terms.

a. porous

b. insulator

c. acid rain

d. fibreglass

e. insoluble

4. Indicate whether the statements are true or false.

a.	A diamond can scratch glass.	True	False
b.	Silver and copper do not get tarnished when exposed to air for a long time.	True	False
c.	Good quality sunglasses totally cut off infrared rays, which are harmful to the eye.	True	False
d.	Steel is harder than a diamond.	True	False
e.	Aerated soft drinks contain dissolved carbon dioxide.	True	False

5. Project Work

In the table, list as many objects as you can that are made of the materials listed in the first column.

Material	Objects made of this material
paper	
wood	
plastic	
iron/steel	
cotton	
leather	
wool	

Do you get an idea of which material is used most widely?

Think it over

1. **Iron has greater density than water but ships made of iron float on water. Why?**
2. **What keeps the water in earthen pots cool in summer?**

5 Separation of Substances

The materials we use in our daily lives are obtained from various sources. They often occur combined with other substances and not in the pure form. Before a substance is used, it is necessary to separate harmful or non-useful substances that may be mixed with it. Sometimes, even useful components need to be separated if they are to be used separately. The substances to be separated may be particles of different sizes or materials. These may be solids, liquids or even gases. Different processes are used for separating substances with different properties mixed together.

Food grains, such as rice and wheat, grow on plants enclosed in husk, which cannot be eaten in that form. So to get edible rice or wheat, the husk has to be removed and separated from the grains. The husk is not consumed by humans. Milk contains fat, which is separated and converted into butter by churning. Both butter and buttermilk are edible and consumed by humans. Rice sometimes has tiny stone chips mixed with it. The stone chips can only be separated by tedious handpicking. Suspended matter in water can be separated by filtering, as is done to separate tea leaves from brewed tea.

Factastic

Whole milk or full-cream milk must have at least 3.5% milk fats in order to be termed as 'whole'. Toned milk, also called single-toned milk, contains a minimum of 3.0% fat while double-toned milk refers to milk with a minimum of 1.5% fat.

husk: seed coverings and small pieces of stem that are separated from the seeds
buttermilk: the liquid remaining after the separation of butter from sour raw milk

Methods of separation

Handpicking

Handpicking can be conveniently used for separating medium-sized solid impurities such as pieces of dirt, stone and husk from wheat, rice or pulses. The quantity of such impurities is usually not very large. Handpicking is also useful while sorting fruits, such as apples and oranges, into different sizes for selling.

Threshing

Manual threshing

Food grains, such as rice and wheat, grow on stalks, which are harvested after the crop is ripe and ready. After harvesting, the stalks are dried in the sun before the grain is separated from them. Each stalk has many grain seeds attached to it which have to be separated from the husk and straw. This is done by threshing. In this process, the stalks are beaten to free the grain seeds. Sometimes, threshing is done with the help of bullocks in fields. Modern methods involve the use of machines to thresh large quantities of grain. Threshing removes the husk from the grain but the free grains are still mixed with the separated husk or chaff, which need to be separated. This is done by a process called winnowing.

Mechanical threshing

Factastic

Early threshing machines were hand-fed and horse-powered and were the size of an upright piano.

Winnowing

Wind winnowing is an ancient agricultural method used for separating grain from chaff. Winnowing is a technique to separate two solid components, one of which is heavier than the other, from a mixture using wind or by blowing air. In its simplest form, it involves throwing the mixture of grain and chaff into the air. The lighter husk particles are blown away by the wind. The seeds of grain get separated and fall down forming a heap. The separated husk is used for many purposes such as fodder for cattle or for fuel.

Circle Time

Visit a village during the wheat or paddy harvesting season and watch how threshing and winnowing are done. Discuss in class how the process can be further modified to increase efficiency.

Sieving and filtering

Food grains and spices often come mixed with dust, dirt and small stones. A sieve is a wire mesh that lets through the small particles while keeping the larger ones behind. It can be used to separate the dust or dirt from grains and spices. In a flour mill, impurities, such as husk and stones, are separated from the wheat grains using a sieve. Usually, a bagful of wheat is poured on a slanting sieve. The impurities pass through the mesh and the grains are collected on top. The process of sieving removes small pieces of stones, stalk and husk that remain with grains of wheat after threshing and winnowing. After the impurities are removed, the wheat grains are ground into flour.

Circle Time

Visit a wholesaler's godown and find out how wheat, rice, pulses and other commodities are cleaned before packing. Discuss the process in class and see if you can come up with other innovative methods that can be used for the purpose.

Gardeners often sieve the soil before planting seeds to remove stone chips and to give the soil a fine texture. Sieving is also used to separate pebbles and stones from sand used at construction sites. Fine suspended matter can be separated from liquids by filtering the liquid mixture through a cloth or filter paper.

Filtering tea leaves

Explore

Milk is a suspension of tiny fat and protein globules in a watery liquid. Whole milk is churned to separate the cream (large fat globules) from skim milk. It is not possible to remove the smaller fat globules and protein in skim milk by filtration.

However, adding a few drops of lemon juice to boiling milk curdles it into solid particles containing protein and fat and an almost clear liquid. The solid particles can be separated from the liquid by filtration. If we pass curdled milk through a sieve or cloth, the solid that gets separated is called *paneer*.

Why does milk curdle into solids and a liquid when lemon juice is added to boiling milk? Find the answer using an encyclopaedia or the internet.

Evaporation

Evaporation of sea water to obtain salt

Almost all the common salt used in the world is obtained from sea water by the process of evaporation. Every litre of sea water contains about 35gm of dissolved salts, most of it being sodium chloride. This salt is separated from sea water by evaporation. When sea water is allowed to stand in shallow evaporation ponds, called salt pans, water gets heated by sunlight and slowly turns into water vapour, through evaporation. In a few days, the water evaporates completely leaving behind the dry solid salts, which is then harvested. Common salt is obtained from this mixture of salts by further purification.

Explore

Take some water from a tube well in a beaker and put it on a burner to boil. Is there any residue left after the water has evaporated? Where did the residue come from?

Now repeat the experiment using distilled water. Do you find any residue?

paneer: cottage cheese made by curdling boiling milk by adding lemon juice and squeezing all the fluids out while collecting the solids
distilled water: water that has been purified by distillation

Separating funnel

Two immiscible liquids can be separated using a funnel. As shown in the diagram, when two immiscible liquids are poured into a funnel, the liquid with a higher density settles at the bottom while the liquid with lower density floats on top. An example of two immiscible liquids is oil and water. Water being heavier than oil, settles at the bottom of the funnel if allowed to stand for a while. The water can then be collected in a container from the bottom of the funnel when the tap of the funnel is opened. Oil which forms the top layer, can also be collected in another container.

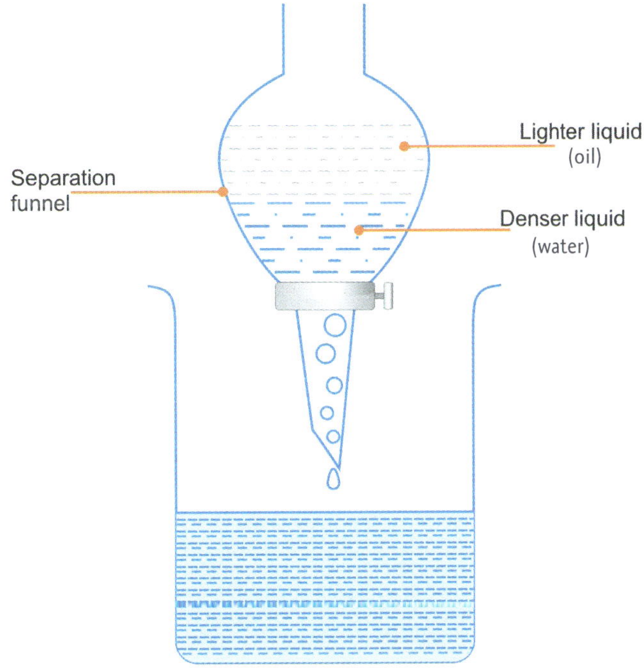

Separation of immiscible liquids

Sedimentation and decantation

Sedimentation
Rice settles at the bottom while foreign particles remain suspended in water.

The process of sedimentation and decantation is used to separate two or more solids that are immiscible in a liquid. Rice and pulses usually come mixed with some dust and sometimes chaff and straw. Therefore, before cooking they are washed. When water is added to the dirty rice and mixed thoroughly, the rice grains sink because they are heavy. This is called sedimentation. The fine dust and other foreign matter remain suspended in the water as they are lighter than water. They can be carefully poured out with the water, leaving the clean rice at the bottom. This process is called **decantation**.

immiscible: incapable of mixing
sedimentation: the process of heavy particles settling at the bottom of a fluid due to gravity
gelatine: a colourless water-soluble protein obtained from animal tissues used to make jelly

Villagers often use alum to purify drinking water. Alum is a double sulphate of potassium and aluminium. Alum breaks up into potassium sulphate, which remains in solution, and aluminium hydroxide, which forms a gelatine-like precipitate when mixed in water. The gelatinous mass settles at the bottom, trapping all the suspended particles in it. The clear water on top can then be decanted and used.

Circle Time

If you happen to live near a coastal town, find out if there are any salt pans nearby and see how salt is separated from water by evaporation.

Separating solids using a magnet

To separate two substances, one of which is made of iron, we can use magnets. For example, to separate iron fillings from sand, we can use a magnet. The iron fillings are attracted to the magnet and, thus, they can be removed from sand and collected in another container.

A combination of methods

While there are several methods by which simple mixtures can be separated in a single step, there may be mixtures that cannot be separated by a single method. Such mixtures would need a combination of two or more methods for complete separation.

For example, it is impossible to separate a simple mixture of sand and salt by any single method such as handpicking or sieving. It would require an indirect method. If water is added to the mixture, the salt will dissolve in it leaving the sand intact. The sand can be separated from the salt solution by the process of decantation or filtration. The salt can then be recovered from the salt solution by evaporating the water by heating. If needed, the water vapour can be turned back into liquid water by cooling. The process is known as condensation. Thus, a mixture of sand, salt and water can be separated by a combination of methods such as decantation, filtration, evaporation and condensation.

Solubility

Many solid substances can dissolve in liquids. The solid substance that we add to the liquid is called the solute and the liquid substance that it is dissolved in, is known as the solvent. The solute and the solvent together form the solution. Many substances are soluble in water; that is, they dissolve when put in water and stirred. Salt and sugar are two common examples. However, a fixed amount of water can dissolve only a certain amount of salt or sugar or any other soluble substance. A solution is said to be saturated when it will not dissolve any more amount of the solute.

Explore

Take a beaker half filled with water. Add salt with a small spoon and stir. Keep adding salt and stir the mixture till no more salt dissolves and the undissolved salt settles at the bottom of the beaker. Place the beaker on a burner. Keep stirring. What happens?

What happens if you keep the hot solution aside to cool slowly?

Apart from the quantity and the temperature of water, how much of a soluble substance can be dissolved in water also depends on the solubility of the substance. Solubility is the quantity of a particular solute that can dissolve in a particular solvent to make a saturated solution.

Explore

Take four small beakers. Put 50 ml of water in each. Take 50 gm each of common salt, sugar, powdered copper sulphate and potassium chloride. Keep adding common salt in small amounts to the water in one beaker and stir constantly till no more salt dissolves. Repeat the same process for the sugar, copper sulphate and potassium chloride samples.

Weigh the common salt, sugar, copper sulphate and potassium chloride that remains. Deduct this amount from the original 50 gm that you had started with. This will give you the amount of each substance that dissolved in the same amount of water to give a saturated solution.

Are the amounts the same? If not, what does it demonstrate?

The dissolving power of water can be used to purify soluble substances such as salt, sugar and many other chemicals. When the impure substance is stirred in water, the soluble part dissolves and the impurities do not. The impurities can be separated by filtration and the solution can then be concentrated and allowed to cool. On cooling, crystals of the pure substance separate out from the saturated solution and can be filtered and then dried. Sugar is extracted from cane juice after chemical treatment by crystallisation. Common salt is also refined by crystallisation.

crystallisation: the formation of crystals

Brainteaser

Tick the items that can dissolve in water.

1. grain of rice	2. salt	3. milk
4. cardamom	5. chilli powder	6. sugar
7. whole gram	8. egg white	9. oil
10. curd		

Answers: 2. salt 3. milk 6. sugar 10. curd

Revision Time

* The materials we use in our daily lives usually occur combined with other substances that need to be separated before use.
* Handpicking, threshing, winnowing, sieving, filtering, sedimentation and decantation are some of the methods commonly used for separating substances from mixtures.
* The difference in the size of particles in a mixture is utilised to separate them by the process of sieving and filtration.
* Filtration can be used to separate the components of a mixture of an insoluble solid and a liquid.
* A saturated solution is one in which no more of a solute can be dissolved.
* The saturation point of a solvent can be increased by heating it.

Quiz Time

1. Answer the questions.

a. What is the minimum fat content of whole milk?

b. What is the process by which wheat is separated from husk and straw known as?

c. By what process can fine suspended matter be separated from liquids?

d. What is a salt pan?

e. How can husk or dirt particles be separated from a given sample of pulses before cooking?

2. Fill in the blanks.

a. Wheat can be separated from husk by ____________.

b. A sieve is usually a ____________ that lets through the small particles while keeping larger ones behind.

c. Milk is a suspension of tiny ____________ and protein globules in a watery liquid.

d. Salt is obtained from sea water by ____________.

e. Water obtained from tube wells is usually ____________ water.

3. Explain the terms.

a. threshing

b. magnetic separation

c. solubility

d. decantation

e. saturated solution

4. Indicate whether the statements are true or false.

a.	Small stone chips can be removed from rice by sieving.	True	False
b.	Winnowing makes use of the wind to separate wheat from husk.	True	False
c.	A fixed amount of water can dissolve only a certain amount of salt.	True	False
d.	Crystals form when a saturated solution is heated.	True	False
e.	The conversion of water vapour into liquid water by cooling is known as condensation.	True	False

5. Activity: Find the words.

Hidden in the grid below are the names of eight methods of separating substances. Find them.

E	O	V	M	W	N	X	I	C
V	T	D	E	C	A	N	T	X
A	Q	U	L	O	B	A	L	K
P	J	O	T	N	E	B	A	N
O	K	E	N	D	A	O	K	C
R	E	P	V	E	K	I	O	E
A	P	I	S	N	O	L	E	V
T	H	R	E	S	H	K	O	I
I	B	S	G	E	S	E	X	J
O	W	I	N	N	O	W	I	L
N	E	F	I	L	T	E	R	S

6. Project Work

In the table below, the first column lists different mixtures that need to be separated into their components. Name the methods to be used for separating the components in the second column.

Mixture	Method(s) to be used
sand and iron filings	
oil and water	
rice, salt and sand	
wheat, husk and dust	

6 Changes Around Us

Changes occur around us constantly. Burning of coal, wood or paper turn them into ash; saplings grow into trees; buds turn into flowers and then into seeds; sugar disappears if put in water and stirred; ice melts into water and then turns into water vapour when heated; dough swells into bread after baking; babies grow into adults; the list is endless.

Any change that occurs can either be a physical change or a chemical change. It may be reversible or irreversible depending on whether or not it is possible to change it back to the original. Changes can be slow or fast, natural or man-made, temporary or permanent.

Physical change

A physical change is the simplest type of change possible. It usually involves a change of state such as the melting of ice into water or the conversion of water into vapour.

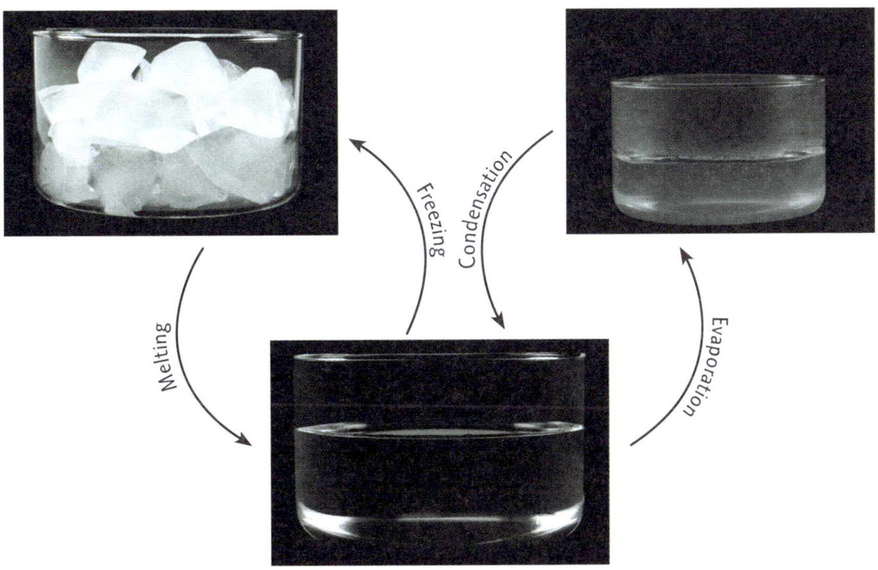

Ice melts to form water and then water vapour which again forms water and can be frozen into ice

Rolling dough into *chapati*

The chemical composition of water (H_2O) remains unchanged in all three states and each can be converted into another.

Dissolving sugar or salt in water involves a physical change because both sugar and salt remain chemically unchanged in the solution and can again be recovered as solid sugar or salt by evaporating the water.

Rolling dough into *chapatis* (without baking), drying a wet cloth, drying wet bricks or pottery and blowing a balloon are all physical changes because the dough, cloth, clay and the balloon remain the same; only their physical shape or state changes.

Drying wet clothes

Blowing a balloon

In a physical change, the constituents of the original object or objects remain unchanged. Most physical changes are reversible; the changes can be undone to bring back the substances to their original states.

Certain physical changes, such as breaking of a glass bottle, cutting of hair or tearing a piece of paper, are irreversible.

Explore

Take some plasticine and make any shape. Can you bring the plasticine back to the original shape. Is this a physical change?

Take an apple. Peel it and cut it into pieces. Can you turn the pieces and the peel back into the original apple? Is this a physical change?

When the pieces of apple are kept on a plate for some time they turn brown. Is this a physical change? Can the brown cut pieces be turned back into white pieces?

Chemical change

Rusted iron nails

Whenever a chemical reaction occurs, the atoms are rearranged and new products are formed. Most chemical changes happen between molecules. For example, the rusting of iron happens over a long period of time and in the process the iron atoms gradually combine with oxygen and become iron oxide molecules, which are reddish brown in colour. The rust cannot be turned back into iron except by a chemical reaction.

If we mix flour, butter, sugar and other ingredients and bake a cake, it would be impossible to separate the various ingredients to their original form. During the process of baking, the ingredients combine and change in a manner that produces new compounds, which give taste and flavour to the cake. Similarly, if coal is burnt, carbon dioxide and water vapour are produced along with the production of heat. The original coal cannot be brought back. That is, the change is irreversible.

Mixing ingredients to bake a cake

Melting of wax

Wax can be melted by heating and the molten wax can be brought back to the solid form by cooling. But when a candle is lighted, the molten wax rising through the wick becomes vapour, which burns, producing light. When a candle burns, it produces carbon dioxide, water vapour and heat, which cannot be recombined to get back solid wax.

A chemical change when accompanied by the production of heat, is known as an **exothermic** reaction. The explosion of dynamite is a violent exothermic reaction. When a chemical reaction is accompanied by the absorption of heat, it is called an **endothermic** reaction.

Explore

With your friends make a few clay articles using wet clay that is used in pottery. Dry the clay articles in the sun. Divide the dried articles into two groups. Fire the clay articles of one group in a wood- or coal- fired kiln and allow them to cool. Take a little water in a bucket. Place the sun-dried clay articles as well as the fired clay articles in water. What do you observe?

Heating expands, cooling shrinks

A simple physical change is observed when solids, liquids and gases are heated. Most solids, liquids and gases expand on heating and contract when cooled. There are some exceptions. Water, for example, shrinks when cooled, but up to a point. If it is cooled below 4°C, it starts expanding and becomes lighter. That is why ice is lighter than water and floats on it. When lakes and rivers freeze in winter, water below the ice layer remains liquid, and fish and other aquatic animals do not die. Also, because water expands on freezing, water pipes sometimes burst in cold places during winter.

The process of the expansion of solids by heating is used by village artisans for making simple tools, such as shovels, *belchas* and digging equipment, used in the field and in construction work. Such tools usually have iron blades with a ring in which the wooden handle is fixed. While making the tool, the diameter of the ring is made slightly smaller in size than the diameter of the wooden handle. When the ring is heated, it becomes slightly larger in size and the wooden handle can be easily pushed in. When the ring cools down, it contracts and fits tightly on to the wooden handle and does not come out easily during use.

Wooden cart with a metal rim on the wheels

A similar technique is used for fixing iron rims on wooden wheels of carts. The iron rim is made slightly smaller than the wooden wheel. Before fitting on the wheel, the rim is heated and pushed over the wheel. Cold water is then poured over the rim, which contracts and fits tightly on to the wheel.

Liquid mercury expands when heated and this property is used to make thermometers. In a thermometer, mercury is stored in a glass bulb at one end of a long glass

capillary: a tube that has an internal diameter of hair-like thinness

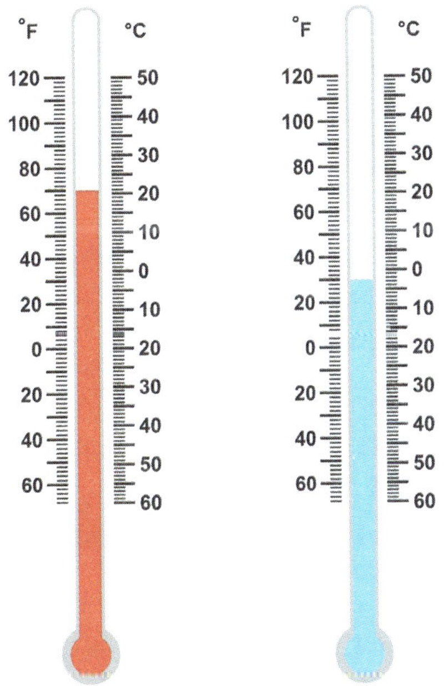

High Temperature   Low Temperature

Thermometers showing mercury levels at low and high temperatures

capillary with thick walls. A scale marked in degrees Celsius or degrees Fahrenheit is marked along the tube. As the temperature rises, mercury in the bulb expands and rises in the capillary. The height up to which the mercury column rises depends on the temperature. The higher the temperature, the greater will be the expansion of mercury and the higher the mercury column in the capillary. When the temperature falls, the opposite action takes place. The volume of mercury in the bulb becomes less and the mercury column in the capillary falls, showing a lower temperature.

Forging and casting

Heating softens and melts metals and this property is used for making metal tools and castings. For making iron tools, a blacksmith first heats the iron piece till it is red hot and becomes soft. The blacksmith then beats the heated piece into the desired shape. Shaping metals by heating and hammering is called forging.

Forging

Heating metals to a high temperature melts them. The molten metal can be poured into moulds to make metal objects such as statues, figurines or candle stands. This process of making metal objects is known as casting. Objects made of metals such as brass, bronze and silver are usually made by casting.

The process of forging and casting metals is a physical change since only the shape of the metal changes.

As is clear from this discussion, there are many ways in which changes occur. Changes can be physical or

forge: make or shape a metal object by heating it in a fire or furnace and hammering it
cast: make an object by pouring molten metal or other material into a mould
brass: a yellow alloy of copper and zinc
bronze: a yellowish-brown alloy of copper with up to one-third tin

Casting

chemical. Some physical changes are reversible. That is, the process can be turned back to obtain the original substances. Chemical changes usually occur at a molecular level and lead to the formation of new molecules and are, therefore, irreversible and cannot be turned back to obtain the original substances. Physical and chemical changes can be put to a wide variety of useful applications.

Revision Time

- Changes occur around us constantly.
- A change can be physical or chemical.
- A change may be reversible or irreversible.
- Physical changes are the simplest type of changes possible.
- In a chemical change, the atoms are rearranged and new products are formed.
- Most solids, liquids and gases expand on heating, which is a physical change.
- Heating softens and melts metals and this property is used for forging and casting metals.
- Shaping metals by heating and hammering is called forging.
- Making metal objects by pouring molten metal into moulds is known as casting.

Quiz Time

1. Answer the questions.

a. Why do sun-dried bricks break up when placed in water but kiln-fired bricks do not?

b. Why does ice float on water?

c. What kind of change is the browning of a cut apple and why?

d. How are the iron rims of wooden cart wheels fitted?

e. What kind of change occurs when an egg is boiled in water?

2. Fill in the blanks.

a. A ________________ change is usually reversible.

b. ________________ of wax is a chemical change.

c. In a chemical change, new ________________ are formed.

d. The rusting of iron is a ________________ change.

e. The explosion of dynamite is an ________________ chemical reaction.

3. Explain the terms.

a. physical change

b. chemical change

c. chemical composition

d. reversible

e. forging

4. Indicate whether the statements are true or false.

a.	Baking of bread is a chemical change.	True	False
b.	The formation of crystals of sugar from a saturated solution is a chemical change.	True	False
c.	All chemical changes are reversible.	True	False
d.	The burning of petrol is a physical change.	True	False
e.	The formation of curd from milk is a reversible change.	True	False

5. Project Work

Look around and identify the changes going on in various places—at home, in school and around you. In the table given on page 64, the first column lists a few commonly observed changes. In the second column mention if the change is reversible or irreversible. Consult an encyclopaedia or the internet if you have any difficulty.

Change	Reversible/Irreversible
milk to curd	
hot milk to cold milk	
atta to *chapati*	
ice to water	
seed to plant	
whole carrot to grated carrot	
dry cement to concrete	
clay to pot	
film to photograph	
egg to omelette	

Activity

Aim: To observe how different solutions freeze.

Material required: water, three clear glass cups, salt, sugar

Method: Mark the three cups as fresh water, salt and sugar. Pour about half a cup of water in each cup. In the cup marked salt, add salt and keep stirring till no more salt dissolves. Repeat the same with sugar. Now keep all the three cups in the freezer overnight to allow the solution inside them to freeze. Observe the three cups the next day. Does the ice look the same in all the three cups? Try poking or scraping them. Is there a difference?

Conclusion: Water molecules arrange themselves in a particular order or pattern when they freeze. However, when salt or sugar is dissolved in the water, they interfere with the regular ice crystal structure. Thus, the frozen liquid is less hard than ice made with fresh water.

Think it over

When water is stored in iron tanks, why do the walls of the tank usually get rusted only around the level of the stored water?

7 Life Around Us

We are surrounded by living and non-living things. All animals and plants are living things while a piece of chalk, sand, wood and glass are non-living things.

Living and non-living

Living things: plants, birds

Living things are those that have life. Human beings, cats, birds, lizards, insects, trees and flowers are all living things because they need food to grow, they grow old and eventually die. On the other hand, chairs, tables, rocks and books are non-living. They have no life. They do not need food to live and do not grow or die.

Non-living things: vehicles, wood

How does one know that something is living? Often, it is not so easy to distinguish between the living and the non-living. Living things possess certain characteristics but they may not hold true for all things that are living. For example, plants are living things, but they do not move like animals. On the other hand, a car or a bus can move, but they are non-living. Plants and animals need food to live and a car or a bus

characteristic: a feature or quality belonging typically to a person, place or thing that serves to identify them

also needs petrol or diesel to run. Plants and animals give off oxygen or carbon dioxide as waste products, while cars and buses emit carbon dioxide, water vapour and other gases as waste. All living organisms appear to grow in size with time, while at times, clouds in the sky or crystals in a solution also grow in size. But cars, clouds and crystals cannot be called living things.

Characteristics of living things

Feeding

Animals cannot make their own food

All living things need to take food from their environment to obtain energy, to grow and to stay healthy.

Plants make their own food through the process of photosynthesis. Animals do not make their own food and depend on their environment including plants and other animals for their food.

Movement

Fish swimming

All living things show movement of one kind or another. All living things have internal movement, which means that they have the ability of moving substances from one part of their body to another. Some living organisms show external movement as well—they can move from place to place by walking, flying, swimming or crawling.

Plants are generally anchored in the soil so they do not move from one place to another. However, various substances, such as, water, minerals and the food synthesised by them, move from one

Bird flying

photosynthesis: the process by which green plants use sunlight to synthesise nutrients from carbon dioxide and water

Insect crawling

part of the plant to the other. Tendrils of some creepers show movement by stretching out and twining around any suitable support nearby. Generally plants bend and grow towards light.

Breathing or respiration

Process of respiration in the presence of sunlight

All living things exchange gases with their environment during the process of respiration. Breathing in and out forms the process of respiration. During respiration, an organism takes in oxygen and releases carbon dioxide.

Respiration is necessary for all living organisms. It is through respiration that the body gets oxygen. Oxygen is necessary for oxidising food to release energy. But not all organisms respire in the same way. For example, earthworms breathe through their skin. Fish have gills that absorb oxygen dissolved in water. The process of respiration in animals, such as cows, buffaloes, dogs and cats, is similar to that in humans. Humans breathe through their nose. The air passes into the lungs where oxygen from the air is absorbed by the lungs to be used by the body while carbon dioxide and unused air are released.

tendril: a slender thread-like appendage of a climbing plant, often growing in a spiral form, which stretches out and twines round any suitable support.

Sapling turning into a tree

Process of respiration at night

Plants use tiny holes mostly in their leaves, known as stomata, for the exchange of gases. Depending on the availability of sunlight, plants respire in two ways. During the day, when photosynthesis occurs, green plants absorb light and carbon dioxide and release oxygen. Sunlight helps break down water within plants and use carbon dioxide to form oxygen and glucose. During the day, the amount of oxygen released by plants in the process of photosynthesis is much more than the oxygen they use for respiration. However, at night in the absence of sunlight, photosynthesis cannot occur, so plants take in oxygen and give off carbon dioxide.

Excretion

Not all the food that is eaten by a living organism is used. Only a part of the broken down food is utilised by the body and the rest has to be removed as waste. All living things need to remove waste from their bodies and they do so by the process of excretion. If this waste is allowed to remain in the body, it could be poisonous. Most animals produce solid waste in the form of faeces as well as liquid waste in the form of urine. They also give off gaseous waste in the form of carbon dioxide during respiration. Certain living beings, such as humans, remove waste products in the form of sweat.

Plants also excrete but the mechanism in plants is a little different. In addition to carbon dioxide and water vapour, some plants produce harmful or poisonous materials as wastes. Some plants store the waste products within their body parts in a way that they do not harm the plant as a whole, but others remove waste products as secretions.

Factastic

The world's oldest living tree is a 9,550-year-old spruce—a conifer—that first took root at the end of the last Ice Age. It was discovered in the Dalarna Province of Sweden in 2004.

Growth

When living things feed, they gain energy, some of which is used in growth. Living things become larger and their bodies and functions become more complex as they grow. Human babies grow into adults; young ones of animals grow into adults; pups grow into dogs; a chick hatched from an egg grows into a hen or a cock; and saplings grow into trees. But living things do not keep growing forever. Each living thing has a certain life span after which it dies.

A chick becomes a hen

A pup grows into a dog

Sensitivity to stimuli

Mimosa plant

Living things react to changes around them. They react to touch, light, heat, cold or sound. Changes in the surroundings that make living things respond to them are called stimuli. Some animals hibernate in winter when the temperature falls. Many insects come out in search of food only during the night. Plants usually grow towards the light. Flowers of some plants bloom only at night. In some plants, flowers close after sunset. Mimosa, commonly known as the 'touch-me-not' plant, has leaves that close or fold when someone touches them.

Sunflower

Reproduction

stimuli: a thing that arouses activity in someone or something and makes it respond

All living things reproduce to form more of their own kind. Humans make babies. Animals also reproduce to make more of their own kind, but the methods may vary in different animals.

An egg hatching into a bird

Birds, lizards, crocodiles and some snakes lay eggs that hatch to produce their young ones. Others such as cows, buffaloes, deer, elephants, dogs and cats give birth to their young ones.

A deer and its young one

An elephant and its young one

Plants also reproduce. Many make seeds that can germinate and grow into new plants. Some plants also reproduce through parts other than seeds. For example, a part of a potato with a bud grows into a new plant; a cutting from a rose or sugarcane plant grows into a full plant. Certain cacti also grow from cuttings.

Seeds are living things. They remain dormant until the conditions become optimal for germination. However, even in the inactive state, seeds carry out metabolic activity such as cellular respiration. In other words, seeds continuously use small amounts of stored energy, staying alive and "waiting" for good conditions to begin to grow. Most

A seed germinating to form a plant

germinate: begin to grow and put out shoots

seeds need water and the correct temperature to begin to grow. Some seeds need special conditions, such as a period of cold weather or may even need to be scorched in a forest fire to begin to grow.

Because living things die, their species can survive over thousands of years only if they reproduce their own kind. In the absence of the process of reproduction, the existence of that organism is not possible.

As mentioned earlier, there are some non-living things, such as cars, buses, trucks, clouds and crystals that also show some of the characteristics of living things. But such things cannot be called living because these objects do not show characteristics such as sensitivity to stimuli and reproduction. Only if an object shows all the characteristics of a living thing at the same time, can it be considered as living.

Non-living but once part of living things

Apart from living and non-living, there is another category of non-living objects that were once living. Fibres, such as cotton, wool and silk, are all obtained from and were once part of living beings. Wood and paper also belong to this category. Coal and oil are also non-living products of once-living organisms.

Explore

Make a list of as many objects as you see around you. Divide them into three groups—living, non-living and non-living but once part of living things. How many non-living things do you find that were once part of living things?

Living organisms and their surroundings

A close examination of animals and plants and their surroundings shows that each is designed specially to live in its particular surroundings or habitat. For example, there is very little water available in deserts. It is very hot during the day and very cold at night in a desert and as a result not many plants grow there. Desert animals have to live on whatever grows in the desert soil. The body structure of a camel helps it survive in such conditions. Camels have long legs, which help keep their bodies away from the heat of the sand. The foot pads of a camel are broad, which makes it easy for them to walk and run on loose sand without sinking. Their mouth is very sturdy and hence they are able to chew thorny desert plants. Long eyelashes and ear hairs, together with sealable nostrils, form a barrier against the blowing sand. Besides, camels excrete very small amounts of urine and their dung is almost dry. Hence, they lose very little water from their bodies and can live for many days without water. No wonder the camel is also known as the 'ship of the desert'.

Plants found in deserts also have certain special characteristics. Their leaves are either totally absent, very small, or present in the shape of spines, which helps in reducing water loss from the leaves through transpiration. The bodies of many cacti are thick and their stems have a waxy coating to prevent the loss of water. Some cacti are in the shape of a sphere or cylinder, which protects them against strong sunlight.

Explore

Take two potted plants—a cactus and a leafy plant. Cover both or parts of both with polythene bags of equal sizes. Place the two pots in the sun and look at the polythene bags after a few hours. Is there any difference in the amount of water collected inside the two polythene bags? What does it show? Which plant loses more water by transpiration?

Fish swimming in water

Fish are found in water—some live in fresh water lakes or rivers while others live in the saline waters of the seas. Fish usually eat tiny plants found in water or larvae of insects. The body of fish is streamlined so that they can move fast in water. They have flat fins and tails that help them to change directions and keep their body balance in water. They also have slippery scales on their bodies, which protect them and help in easy movement through water. Fish also have special organs called gills that help them use oxygen dissolved in water for breathing. They cannot live out of water.

The presence of specific features, such as the broad foot pads of the camel, thick stem and thorns of cacti and gills of fish or certain habits that enable a plant or an animal to live in its surroundings is called an **adaptation**. It is an evolutionary process. Adaptation does not take place in a short time. The environmental factors of a region change over thousands of years. Those animals that cannot adapt to changes die out and only the ones that adapt to the changes in the habitat survive. Animals adapt to different

transpiration: the emission of water vapour from the leaves of plants

environmental factors in different ways, which leads to a variety of organisms present in diverse habitats.

Habitats

A habitat is the natural home or environment of a particular species of animal, plant or any other type of organism. A living thing depends on its habitat for food, water, air, shelter and other needs. Several kinds of plants and animals may share the same habitat.

Habitats can be of different types. **Terrestrial habitats** are found on land and include forests, grasslands, deserts and coastal and mountain regions. However, there are large variations in the terrestrial habitats located in different parts of the world. Aquatic **habitats** include ponds, swamps, lakes, rivers and oceans where many varieties of plant animal life thrive.

Polar bears and a bear in a terrestrial habitat

Aquatic habitats: pond, river and lake

aquatic: of or relating to water

Explore

Look up the internet and books on nature and animals to find out different habitats such as forests, mountains, deserts, ponds and oceans of animals, birds, insects and plants. Make a table with columns labelled with the names of different habitats and put the names of animals, birds, insects and plants in the appropriate columns. Are some animals and plants common to more than one habitat? Do they have any common features?

Every habitat has its biotic and abiotic components. Biotic components are the living things such as plants, animals and other organisms that share the habitat. Abiotic components are made up of non-living things such as rocks, soil, air and water, and also sunlight and heat available in the habitat.

In order to grow and survive, every living organism needs both biotic and abiotic components of its habitat. A common example is the sprouting of seeds. Seeds can be stored for a long time without sprouting if kept completely dry. But if suitable abiotic factors, such as moisture, warmth and air, are available they sprout or germinate, setting off the process of growth, which turns the seed into a complete plant.

Terrestrial habitats

Forests

Many animals and plants live in forests. Most forests have tall trees. Different trees grow in different places. The forest habitat is often cool, moist, dark and shady. Tropical rainforests are humid and warm. They receive a lot of rainfall.

Deciduous trees grow in warm places. They have big leaves that die and fall to the ground in the autumn season. Some living things found in a forest are tigers, deer, wild boars, monkeys, squirrels, woodpeckers, spiders, snails and many others. For their habitat and food, they depend upon other plants and animals that live in the forest with them.

Tiger and deer in a forest habitat

biotic: relating to or resulting from living organisms
abiotic: physical rather than biological; not derived from living organisms

Explore

Take some dry whole *moong* seeds. Keep half aside in a beaker labelled A. Soak the rest in water for a day in a beaker labelled B. Take out one-third of the soaked seeds from Beaker B and keep the rest completely submerged in water for 3-4 days. Divide the soaked seeds into three parts C, D and E. Keep 'C' wrapped in a piece of thin, wet cotton cloth in a well-lighted room. Keep 'D' wrapped in wet cotton cloth in a completely dark place, for example, inside a box or in a cupboard that does not allow any light to come in. Keep 'E', again wrapped in a wet cotton cloth, in a very cold place, say, in a refrigerator or an ice box.

Wait for a couple of days. Look at the seeds in all the five beakers. Have they germinated? Look inside the three cotton wraps that contained soaked seeds. Have they all germinated? What are the abiotic factors you think are necessary for the seeds to germinate?

Forests also constitute the arboreal **habitat** for those animals, such as monkeys, squirrels, snakes and others, that live and make their home on trees.

Mountains

Squirrel and snake in an arboreal habitat

Mountains are usually very cold and windy. In some areas, snowfall takes place in winters. Conifers are trees that are mostly found in mountainous regions. Conifers are normally cone shaped and have sloping branches. They do not have leaves but have needles, which help rainwater and snow slide off easily.

Mountain goat and a bear in a mountain region

arboreal: living on trees

Animals living in the mountain regions are also adapted to cold conditions. They have thick skin or fur to protect them from the cold. Some animals that live on the mountains have strong hooves for running up the rocky slopes of mountains.

Deserts

Deserts are extremely dry places, which get very hot during the day and very cold during the night. As discussed earlier, a camel is well adapted to living in a desert as are cacti. There are other animals and plants found in deserts that have also adapted to desert life. Desert animals, such as rats and snakes burrow deep in the sand during the day to stay away from the intense daytime heat. These animals come out at night, when it is cooler.

Camels in a desert

Plants too, have adapted to survive in the harsh conditions of the hot deserts. Most desert plants have modified leaves in the form of spines. This helps to prevent the loss of water through **transpiration**. Photosynthesis in these plants is usually carried out in the stems, which are covered with a thick waxy layer that helps retain water. Most desert plants have roots that go very deep into the soil for absorbing water.

Factastic

A fully grown tree may lose a few cubic metres of water through its leaves on a hot, dry day. About 90% of the water that enters a plant's roots is lost through transpiration.

Temperate or cold deserts are seen in the temperate regions at higher altitudes. These deserts, also known as polar deserts, are covered in snow and have extremely cold temperatures throughout the year. The Arctic and Antarctic regions are cold deserts. Penguins live in Antarctica and swim in the icy cold waters or live on snow-covered land. Blue whales are found in colder areas. Few plants grow in cold deserts and include mosses, grasses and herbs.

Grasslands

A grassland

Grasslands can be defined as grass-dominated areas where few or no trees grow and include the Prairies and the Savannas. They are one of the most endangered ecosystems in the world. Grasslands are full of life, with many animals that rely on the abundant resources of grasslands to provide them with food, shelter and a place to reproduce.

Butterflies and beetles in grasslands

Lions in grasslands

The diversity of plant species found in grasslands allows a wide variety of plant-eating insects to thrive. The fact that most of the plants are grasses means that grass-eating herbivores in particular can be found in this kind of habitat. Grasslands are also home to many butterflies as well as grasshoppers, crickets, ants, lady birds, dragonflies, damselflies and many other fly and beetle species. Some grasslands are home to predators, such as lions, which kill and prey on plant-eating animals, such as the deer.

Aquatic habitats

Rivers, ponds and lakes

Rivers, ponds and lakes are freshwater bodies that harbour a wide variety of plants and

Frog and fish in an aquatic habitat

aquatic life. Water plants, such as lotus and lily, usually have their roots fixed in the soil under the water. The stems of these plants are long, hollow and light, and grow up to the surface of water. The leaves and flowers float on the surface of the water. But some plants, such as the water hyacinth, are free-floating. They have long, spongy and bulbous stalks and feathery, freely hanging roots.

Some aquatic plants remain totally submerged in water. All parts of such plants grow under water. Some of these plants have narrow and thin ribbon-like leaves, which can bend in the flowing water. In some submerged plants, leaves are often highly divided, through which the water can easily flow without damaging them.

Freshwater lakes and ponds are home to a wide variety of frogs and fishes, which live on insects, insect larvae or plant parts found in the water.

Oceans

Oceans and seas contain salty water and are home to a large number of fishes and other animals. As stated earlier, the body of a fish is designed such that it can move fast in water and use oxygen dissolved in water.

Animals on an ocean floor

Some sea animals, such as squids and octopuses, do not have a streamlined body like fishes. However, when they move in water, they make their body shapes streamlined. These animals also breathe with gills, using oxygen dissolved in water. They usually live at great depths in the ocean, close to the ocean floor and catch any prey that moves towards them.

Besides fish, which can breathe under water, there are some sea animals, such as dolphins and whales, which do not have gills. They breathe in air through nostrils or blowholes that are located on the upper parts of their heads. These animals, which are actually mammals, have to come to the surface to breathe in air. They can stay under water for long periods of time without breathing.

Corals in an ocean

The oceans are also home to a group of tiny organisms, the skeletons of which build up colourful underwater structures known as corals.

Brainteaser

Some animals and their typical features are mentioned below. One of the options is incorrect. Cross out the incorrect option.

1. Frogs
   - a. live on land and water.
   - b. have scales.
   - c. eat insects.
   - d. have a long tongue
2. Polar bears
   - a. have strong limbs.
   - b. eat fish.
   - c. have fur.
   - d. have very light bodies.
3. Fishes have
   - a. scales.
   - b. fins.
   - c. gills.
   - d. claws.
4. Whales have
   - a. tails.
   - b. blubber.
   - c. fur.
   - d. lungs.
5. Birds have
   - a. wings.
   - b. very light bodies.
   - c. feathers.
   - d. gills.

Answers: 1. have scales 2. have very light bodies 3. claws 4. fur 5. gills

Revision Time

- ✶ We are surrounded by living and non-living things.
- ✶ All living organisms show characteristics, such as feeding, movement, respiration, excretion, sensitivity to stimuli, growth and reproduction.
- ✶ Objects that do not show all the characteristics of living things are considered non-living.
- ✶ Apart from living and non-living things, there is another category of non-living objects, such as cotton, wool, silk, which were once part of living things.
- ✶ Plants and animals adapt to different environmental factors in different ways.
- ✶ A habitat is the natural home or environment of a particular species of animal, plant or any other organism.
- ✶ Habitats can be terrestrial or aquatic.
- ✶ Terrestrial habitats include forests, mountains, deserts and grasslands.
- ✶ Aquatic habitats include rivers, ponds, lakes and oceans.
- ✶ Every habitat has its biotic and abiotic components.

Quiz Time

1. Answer the questions.

a. What differentiates the living from the non-living?

b. Why is respiration necessary for all living beings?

c. What are the characteristics of desert plants that help them conserve water?

d. Forests, grasslands, deserts, coastal and mountain regions belong to which type of habitat?

e. What are the abiotic components of a habitat?

2. Fill in the blanks.

a. Camels and cacti are found in the ____________________ habitat.

b. Dolphins and whales breathe air like ____________________.

c. Ponds, lakes and oceans form the ____________________ habitat.

d. Fish, octopuses and squids breathe through ____________________.

e. Conifers have ____________________, which help rainwater and snow to slide off easily.

3. Explain the terms.

a. habitat

b. respiration

c. aquatic

d. deciduous

e. conifers

4. Indicate whether the statements are true or false.

a.	Dolphins breathe with gills using oxygen dissolved in water.	True	False
b.	All living things reproduce.	True	False
c.	Some aquatic plants remain totally submerged in water.	True	False
d.	Animals living in the mountain regions have thin skin or fur.	True	False
e.	The grasslands are one of the most endangered ecosystems in the world.	True	False

5. Project Work

In the table, the first column lists animals and plants found in different habitats. You may add more. Fill the second column with the appropriate name of the habitat in which they are found.

Organism	Habitat
lion	
tiger	
camel	
rattlesnake	
crocodile	
whale	
snow leopard	
musk deer	
pashmina goat	
starfish	
corals	

Think it over

What characteristics make the yak ideally suited for life in an extremely cold climate?

8 Understanding Plants

Plants play a vital role in the maintenance of life on earth. Plants are the only life forms that can produce their own food using energy from sunlight. Not only do we depend on plants for food, we also depend on them for fuel, shelter, etc. Plants transform radiant energy from the sun into organic chemical energy in the form of sugars, starch and other products. Human beings and animals consume the fruits, flowers, roots, leaves, stems and seeds of plants. Wheat and rice are grown all over the world and are the staple diet of most people. Without these important food items, people's lives would be very different. The seeds of these plants are good to eat, full of nutrients and can be made into many different food items.

Wheat plants

Rice plants

For centuries, plants have been one of the most useful natural resources in the world. They are used for building houses, making clothes, as fuel, among other things.

Plants produce almost all of the oxygen in the air that humans and other animals breathe. Apart from their commercial and aesthetic value, plants conserve other natural resources by protecting soil from erosion, by controlling water levels and quality, and by producing a favourable atmosphere.

There are about 300,000 plant species on earth. Plants come in a wide variety of shapes and sizes. Some are small, some very big, while some are just patches of green on the soil.

Some plants have green leaves, while some others have reddish ones. Some have large flowers, some have tiny ones, while some do not produce any flowers at all.

Circle Time

Discuss with your friends the types of plants that they have seen in their neighbourhood. Try and find their names and write a brief description of these plants.

Herb

Plants are often classified according to their size, structure and nature of their stems. Plants with green and tender stems, such as coriander and mint, are called **herbs**. They are usually short and do not have many branches. Some flowering plants, such as hibiscus and poinsettia, have stems that branch out near the ground. The stem is hard but not very thick. Such plants are called **shrubs**. Some plants, such as peepal and neem, are very tall and have a single hard and thick brown stem or trunk that grows to a considerable height. They bear branches that grow at some height from the ground. Such plants are called **trees**.

Shrub

Tree

Some plants with weak stems cannot stand upright and grow along the ground, around other plants, or up a wall by means of extending stems or branches. Such plants are called **creepers**. Plants with weak stems that take support from nearby structures, such as walls or trees, and climb up are known as **climbers**.

Climber

Moss

Besides the categories mentioned here there is also **moss**—a small, flowerless green plant that commonly grows close together in clumps or mats in damp or shady locations—and **grass**—typically a short plant with long, narrow leaves growing wild or cultivated on lawns and as a fodder crop. There are also water plants, such as water lily, lotus and certain aquarium plants, that grow in or under water.

Grass

Explore

Look closely at the stems and branches of as many plants that you find in and around your school and neighbourhood. Look at their sizes, colours and structures and examine from where the branches grow. Feel their stems and try to bend them gently to see if they are tender or hard. If you know the names of the plants, group them as herbs, shrubs and trees, according to what you find about their size, colour and structure. If you don't know the name, consult an encyclopaedia or look up the internet to identify the plant.

Parts of a plant

Every plant has well-defined parts—root, stem, leaves and flowers. Typically, plants have two parts—an underground part that consists of the root system and the parts that are above the ground that consist of the shoot system, which includes the stem, leaves and flowers.

Root

fodder: food, especially dried hay or straw, for cattle and other livestock

The root is an important part of a plant that typically lies below the surface of the soil. It grips the plant to the soil and helps the plant to absorb water and nutrients from the soil. There

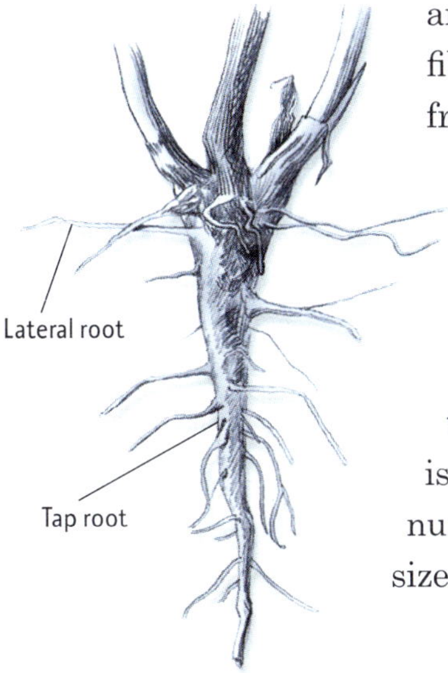

Tap root system

are two main types of roots—tap roots and fibrous roots. The first root that emerges from a seed is called the radicle. In many plants, this root greatly enlarges to become the most prominent root of the plant and is known as a **tap root**. Many smaller branch roots, called **lateral roots**, grow from the tap root. In some plants, the radicle is short-lived and is replaced by numerous roots of more or less equal size. These are known as fibrous **roots**.

Fibrous root system

Some plants, such as sugar cane, have their roots entirely above the ground. Such roots are called **aerial roots**. In some plants, such as the banyan tree, the aerial roots are called **prop roots** because they support the plant. In some plants, such as strawberry, roots help produce new plants. Roots of plants, such as radish, beet, turnip and carrot, store food and nutrients.

Aerial roots

Factastic

In a full-grown rye plant, the total length of the root could reach 613 km.

Explore

Collect small flower pots and fill them with loose soil. Dig out weeds growing in the school backyard, taking care not to damage the roots. Select plants of the same size as far as possible. Divide the weeds into two groups. Plant weeds with roots intact in one set of pots. In another set of pots, plant the weeds after cutting off their roots. Water both sets of pots regularly and observe the plants after a week. Is there any difference between the plants in the two sets of pots?

fibrous: consisting of or characterised by fibres
weed: a wild plant growing where it is not wanted

Stem

Usually found above the ground, the stem bears branches, leaves, flowers and fruits. The main function of the stem is to carry nutrients and water to the different parts of the plant. The stem contains a series of thin tubes called xylem through which water and other nutrients move up by capillary action. Transpiration, or escape of water through tiny pores in leaves, also helps in the transport of water and nutrients from the roots to the top. The stem also carries the food prepared in the leaves by photosynthesis to other parts of the plant including the roots. The stem is usually divided into nodes and internodes. The node is the part of a plant stem that holds buds from which one or more leaves, flowers or other stems emerge, often forming a slight swelling or knob. The internode is the part of a plant stem between two nodes.

Nodes and internodes

Factastic

Bamboos are the fastest growing woody plants in the world. They are capable of growing up to 60 cm or more in a day.

The stem (or trunk) and the distribution of its branches give a plant its characteristic shape. The stem helps in holding the leaves such that they get enough sunlight to carry out the process of photosynthesis. Certain stems that are green in colour can carry out photosynthesis themselves.

Some stems in certain plants are modified to carry out specific functions. For example, in a cactus plant, the stem is green and performs photosynthesis like a leaf. Other modified stems include tubers (potato), rhizomes (ginger) and bulbs (onion and garlic) that grow underground and store food. Stem tendrils are modified stems. They are slender, spirally coiling sensitive organs serving to attach a climbing plant to its support. The grape vine has stem tendrils.

xylem: the thin, tube-like tissue in plants, which conducts water and dissolved nutrients upwards from the root and also helps to form the woody element in the stem
capillary action: the movement of a liquid through thin tubes or porous material, as a result of surface tension
transpiration: the release of water vapour through tiny pores in leaves

Stem tendrils

Circle Time

Initiate a discussion on the uses of stems. The stems of which plants are useful to humans?

Leaf

The leaf is one of the most important part of a plant because it performs the functions of photosynthesis, respiration and transpiration. The green colour of leaves is due to the presence of a pigment called chlorophyll, which makes it possible for leaves to use sunlight and turn carbon dioxide from air and water into carbohydrates by a process called **photosynthesis**. The carbohydrates prepared by the leaves is used for providing energy to all parts of the plant. The excess carbohydrates are stored as starch in different parts of the plant. Oxygen is produced as a by-product of photosynthesis and is released by the plant during this process.

Explore

Take any plant with white flowers that grow on a long stalk. Cut the stem with flowers carefully with a sharp blade. Half fill a glass with water. Add a few drops of red ink to the water and mix it thoroughly.

Put the cut stem with white flowers in the glass so that the cut end is well under water. Wait about twenty-four hours and then look at the flowers. Is there any change in their colour?

Cut the flower stalk across and look closely with a magnifying glass. What do you find? You can also do the same activity with a celery stick.

A simple leaf

Leaves differ widely in shape, size and colour, which help us distinguish between different kinds of plants. However, essentially every leaf has two well-defined parts called the blade and the petiole. The blade is the expanded part of the leaf, which is the most clearly visible part. The petiole is the part of the leaf that connects the blade to the stem.

Activity

Aim: To demonstrate the presence of starch in green leaves that have been kept in the sunlight.

Material required: a green potted plant, iodine solution and black paper

Method: Take a large-leafed potted plant that has been kept in a dark room for a day or two. Cover half a leaf completely with black paper and leave the plant in the sun for a day. Take the plant indoors and remove the leaf partially covered in black paper from the plant. Cut out the covered portion of the leaf and test for starch using iodine solution. Test the uncovered portion of the leaf for starch in the same way. What do you find? Does the covered portion contain starch? What does this experiment tell you about the role of sunlight in photosynthesis?

Conclusion: ______________________________

In all leaves there is a thick vein in the middle of the leaf, which is called the midrib from which other veins branch out. The arrangement of veins in a leaf is called the **leaf venation**. If it is net-like on both sides of midrib, as found in a peepal leaf, the venation is called **reticulate venation**. If the veins are parallel to one another, as found in grass or maize plants, the venation is called **parallel venation**.

Reticulate venation in a leaf

Parallel venation in a leaf

Explore

Collect whole plants of gram, tomato, brinjal, maize, wheat and rice along with roots. Wash off the soil from the roots. Examine the leaves and roots of each. Observe which plants have tap roots and which ones have fibrous roots.

Do you find any correlation between the arrangement of veins in a leaf and the root type? Is it possible to tell the type of root a plant has from the kind of venation of its leaf?

Leaves have tiny pores called stomata that open and close to allow the movement of gases in and out of the leaf cells. Carbon dioxide from air enters the leaf and oxygen is released. Plants also lose a lot of water through the stomata—a process called **transpiration**. Transpiration helps in cooling the

stomata: minute pores in a leaf through which gases and water vapour can pass

plant and enables the flow of mineral, nutrients and water from roots to the rest of the plant.

Spines in cactus

Tendrils in leaves

Leaves of certain plants, such as cacti, are modified to form spines. Spines reduce the loss of water from the plants and also protect it from grazing animals. Some leaves of the pea plant are modified to form tendrils.

Explore

Take a small, well-watered potted plant. Take two transparent polythene bags of equal size. In one, enclose a leafy branch of the plant and tie the bag at the mouth. Keep the plant with the bag in the sun. Tie the mouth of the other polythene bag and also keep it in the sun.

After a few hours, look inside the polythene bags carefully. Is there any difference between them? In which polythene bag do you find droplets of water? How did they get there?

Flowers

Most plants produce flowers mainly for reproduction. Flowers produce seeds from which new plants can grow. Flowers of most plants are colourful and fragrant which helps to attract pollinators, such as insects, birds and bats to them. These pollinators play an important role in the process of pollination.

Factastic

The flower of *Rafflesia arnoldii*, found in the rainforests of Indonesia, is the largest in the world and attains a diameter of nearly 1 m and can weigh up to 11 kg. When in bloom, the *Rafflesia* flower emits a repulsive odour, similar to that of rotting meat. This odour attracts insects that pollinate the plant.

Flowers come in a wide variety of shapes and sizes, but they all have almost similar parts. They are made up of the calyx, corolla, androecium and gynoecium. Before a flower blooms, it is in the form of a bud in which all the parts are enclosed in a green cover called the **calyx**. The calyx is made up of leaf-like structures called the sepals. When the bud develops into

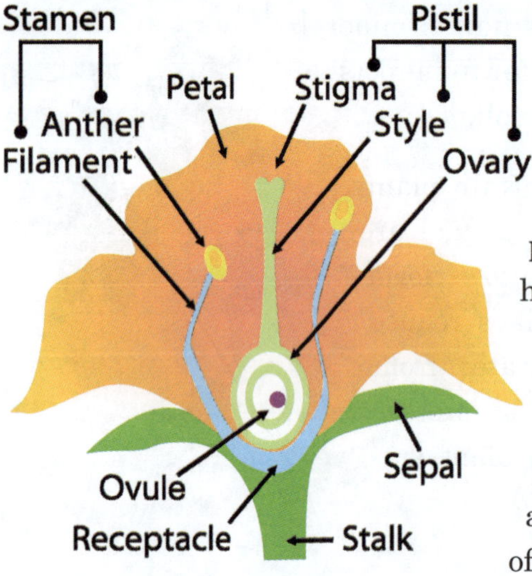

a flower, the **sepals** open up. Enclosed within are the most prominent parts of a flower—the **petals**. Different flowers have petals of different shapes and colours. Some flowers have a fixed number of petals while in others the number of petals varies. In some flowers, such as petunia and *datura*, the petals are not separate but joined together in the shape of a trumpet. The petals of a flower are typically in a concentric shape called **corolla**, which enclose the reproductive organs.

Trumpet-shaped flower

The gynoecium is the female part of the flower and consists of the **pistil**. The pistil usually has a sack at its base called the **ovary**, which contains the female germ cells of a plant or **ovules**. Ovules develop into seeds after fertilisation. Coming out of the ovary is a column called the **style**, which is crowned by a sticky structure called the **stigma**; the stickiness makes the stigma suitable for receiving and retaining pollen grains.

The pistil is nearly surrounded by the androecium, the male parts of the flower, which are called the **stamens**. Each stamen consists of a slender stalk, called the **filament**, topped by an enlarged structure called the **anther**. It is the anther that carries the pollen grains.

After pollination, when pollens reach the ovary at the centre of the flower, fertilisation takes place, which leads to the formation of fruits and seeds. Seeds germinate to form plants.

Factastic

The tiny flowers of the fig tree cannot be seen because they remain inside the green figs that we eat as fruits.

The flowers that are pollinated by insects are usually colourful and attractive and have additional structures called nectaries, which secrete sugary nectar and thus attract insects to the flowers. In their search for nectar, the insects often push against the anthers causing the pollen

pollen: a fine powdery substance, typically yellow, consisting of microscopic grains discharged from the male part of a flower

nectary: a nectar-secreting organ in a flower

Insect pollination

grains to get stuck on their bodies. These pollen grains may then brush off on the stigma of the next flower that the insect visits and in this way flowers are pollinated.

Wind pollination is also common in flowering plants. The flowers of plants pollinated by the wind are usually not colourful. They also do not produce nectar or any scent as they do not need to attract insects. Wind-pollinated plants usually produce large quantities of pollen.

Wind pollination

Circle Time

Collect buds and flowers of different types, for example, rose, petunia, *datura*, nasturtium, lily, tomato, dahlia, hibiscus and any others you can get easily. Study each flower carefully. Do all of them have all the parts mentioned above? Do the flowers differ much in their overall shape? Identify the different parts of each flower and see if they differ in shape and size. Open up the buds carefully and find out how the petals are arranged. Complete the table.

Name of flower	Colour	Number of petals	Number and colour of sepals	Number of stamens	Pistil present/absent

Make drawings of all the parts of the flowers that you may have seen.

Although most flowers have both the male (stamen) and the female (pistil) parts, some plants, such as the papaya, produce two types of flowers—male and female—and only the plants that produce female flowers can bear fruit.

Male and female flowers in a papaya plant

Brainteaser

We obtain a lot of things from different parts of a plant. Identify the plant part from where we get the following items.

1. tea	leaves	2. rubber	________
3. sugar	________	4. paper	________
5. perfume	________	6. cooking oil	________
7. wood	________	8. coffee	________
9. jute	________	10. eucalyptus oil	________

Answers: 2. stem 3. stem 4. stem 5. flower 6. seed 7. stem 8. seed 9. stem 10. leaf

Quiz Time

1. Answer the questions.

a. What gives green colour to leaves?

b. Which types of roots do radish, carrot and turnip have?

c. What substance is produced by green leaves during photosynthesis?

d. Which part of a plant absorbs water and nutrients from the soil?

e. What role do flowers play in the life of a plant?

2. Fill in the blanks.

a. Plants with green and tender stems, such as coriander and mint, are called ______________.

b. Mosses are small ______________ green plants that commonly grow close together in clumps or mats in damp or shady locations.

c. Smaller branch roots growing from a tap root are called ______________ roots.

d. ______________ is the part of a plant stem from which one or more leaves emerge, often forming a slight swelling or knob.

e. Leaves have tiny pores called ______________, that open and close to allow the movement of gases in and out of the leaf cells.

3. Indicate whether the statements are true or false.

a.	Plants are the only life forms that can produce their own food.	True	False
b.	Plants produce almost all of the oxygen in the air that humans and other animals breathe.	True	False
c.	Maize and rice plants have tap roots.	True	False
d.	The stem carries the food prepared in leaves by photosynthesis to other parts of the plant including the roots.	True	False
e.	A peepal leaf shows parallel venation.	True	False

4. Explain the terms.

a. corolla

b. internode

c. photosynthesis

d. radicle

e. xylem

5. Project Work

a. In the first column of the table given on the next page, enter the names of some common plants. Examine them carefully. Fill up the rest of the columns on the basis of your observations as per the example given.

Plant name	Height	Nature of stem (tender, thick, hard)	Branching (near the ground, higher up)	Category of plant
Mint (*Pudina*)	20 cm	Tender	Near the ground	Herb

Think it over

Why do green leaves turn brown, yellow or red before falling in autumn?

9 How Animals Move

Movement is one of the main characteristics of living beings—from microscopic bacteria and tiny insects to birds, fish, giant mammals and humans. Every animal is equipped with special organs for movement and has its own style of moving from one place to another. Bacteria wiggle around in a liquid using tiny appendages called cilia. Insects crawl and fly; birds fly; fish swim; snakes slither; and mammals including humans walk or run. Animals can also perform certain movements while in one place such as eating food, which requires the movement of the mouth and hands, nodding their heads and using their hands and fingers for other activities.

Explore

Make a list of animals. Include mammals, birds, fish, insects, reptiles and snakes in your list. Find out how they move by observing them or by collecting information from the internet or an encyclopaedia.

Do you find anything unusual? Do all birds fly? Are all animals that fly birds? Can all animals that live in water and swim be called fish?

Animals can be divided into two groups—vertebrates and invertebrates. Animals with backbones are called vertebrates, while animals without backbones called invertebrates. Bones give shape to the body. Bones and muscles help vertebrates in moving their limbs and assist in activities such as walking, running, jumping and climbing. Invertebrates use other means to move from one place to another.

The human body

The human body is made of bone, joints and muscles that makes movement possible. Apart from the movement of the human body from one place to the other, movement is also seen when you laugh, talk, write, eat,

vertebrates: animals with backbones

drink, turn or move your head. Even when the human body appears to be still, there are several things that are moving within it. The heart beats continuously while the lungs expand and contract during breathing. Internal movement goes on even when you walk, run and even sleep. Different joints and muscles of the body are used for various activities.

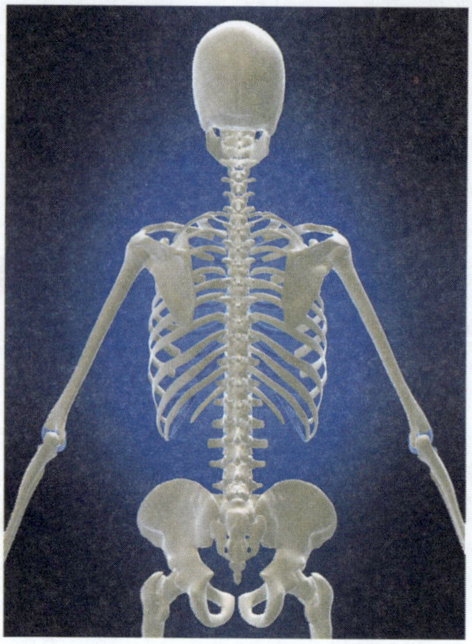

Human skeleton

Bones

Bones form the framework of the human body. They provide support and shape to the body. Although they are very light, bones are strong enough to support our entire body weight.

Table 9.1 Functions of specific bones

Bone	Body part that it protects
Skull	protects the brain that is enclosed within it and gives shape to the face.
Backbone or the spine	makes it possible for humans to stand upright. It protects the spinal cord, which carries nerve impulses to and from the brain to the rest of the body and also carries signals of touch, heat, smell, etc., to the brain.
Ribs and rib cage	shelter the heart, lungs, liver and spleen.
Pelvis	protects the bladder and intestines and the reproductive organs in women.

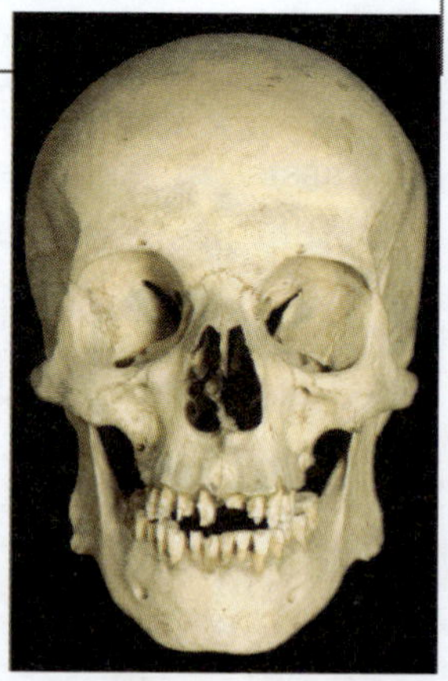

Human skull

The human **skull** or the cranium is made of many bones joined together that seem like one. It has holes for the eyes, nose, ears and mouth. The only part of the skull that is movable is the lower **jawbone**, also known as the mandible.

The skull encloses and protects the brain. It sits at the top of a flexible bony column called the **spine** or **backbone**. Each part of the backbone is called a **vertebra**. There are thirty-

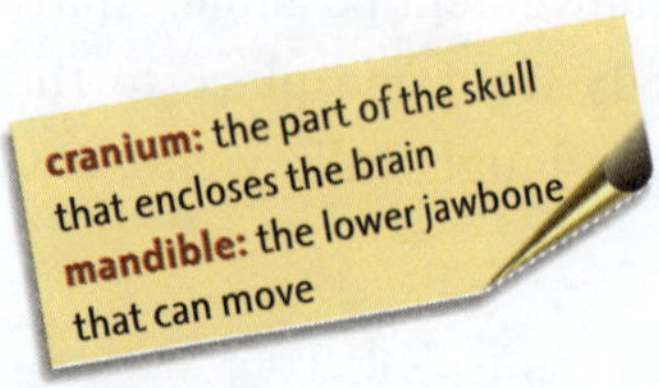

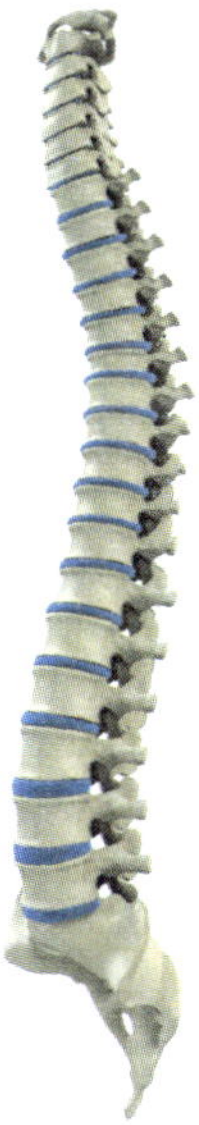
Human spine

three vertebrae in the human backbone joined together in such a way that the backbone is able to bend forward, backward and sideways to some extent. Joined to the upper part of the backbone is a cage-like structure formed by curved strips of bones called **ribs**. There are twenty-four ribs arranged in twelve pairs and all are joined to the backbone. Many important organs of the body, such as the heart and lungs, are enclosed in and protected by the rib cage. Parts of the stomach and the kidneys are also protected by the **rib cage**.

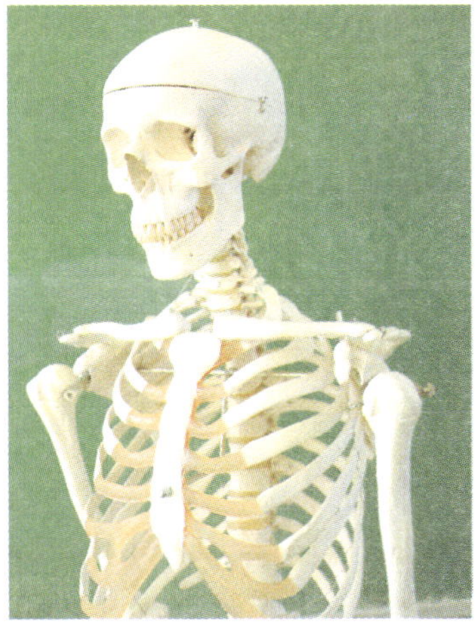
Human ribcage

The two almost horizontal bones over the top of the chest are called **clavicles** or **collarbones**. These can be easily felt by touching since they are not covered with muscle but only with skin.

Each human arm is made up of three long bones joined at the elbow and many small bones that make up the palm and fingers. The upper arm has a single bone called the humerus, which extends from the shoulder to the elbow. The lower arm has two bones—the radius and the ulna.

Factastic

The strongest bone in the human body is the thigh bone, which is stronger than concrete, but is hollow.

In the same way, each human leg is made up of three long bones and many smaller bones that make up the foot. The upper part of the leg, from the hip to the knee, is made up off a single thick bone called the femur while the lower part of the leg has two bones—the tibia and **fibula**. The femur or the thigh bone is the longest bone in the human body.

humerus: the bone extending from the shoulder to the elbow
radius: the outer and slightly shorter of the two bones of the human forearm
ulna: the inner and longer of the two bones of the human forearm
femur: the longest and thickest bone of the human skeleton, which extends from the pelvis to the knee
tibia: the inner and thicker of the two bones of the human leg between the knee and the ankle
coccyx: the lower end of the backbone in humans and tailless apes

Humans do not have tails, but at the lower end of the backbone there is a tiny pointed region known as the coccyx, which is believed to be the residual part of an undeveloped tail.

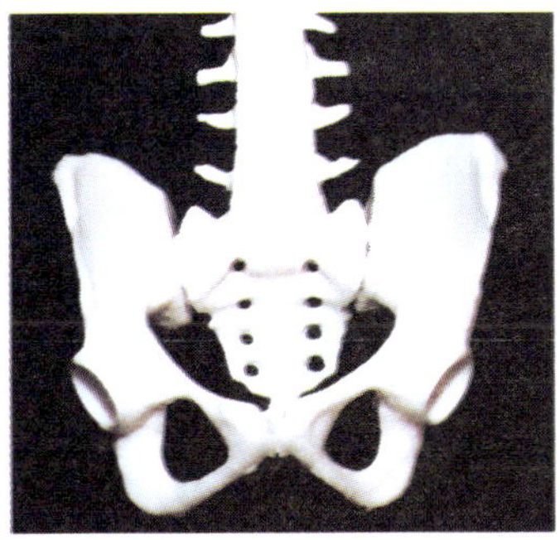
Human pelvis

The lower end of the backbone is attached to the **pelvis** or hip bones that support the legs in humans.

Explore

Label the bones listed here on the diagram of the human skeleton.

cranium

mandible

pelvis

clavicle

tibia

rib cage

vertebrae

coccyx

femur

humerus

radius

ulna

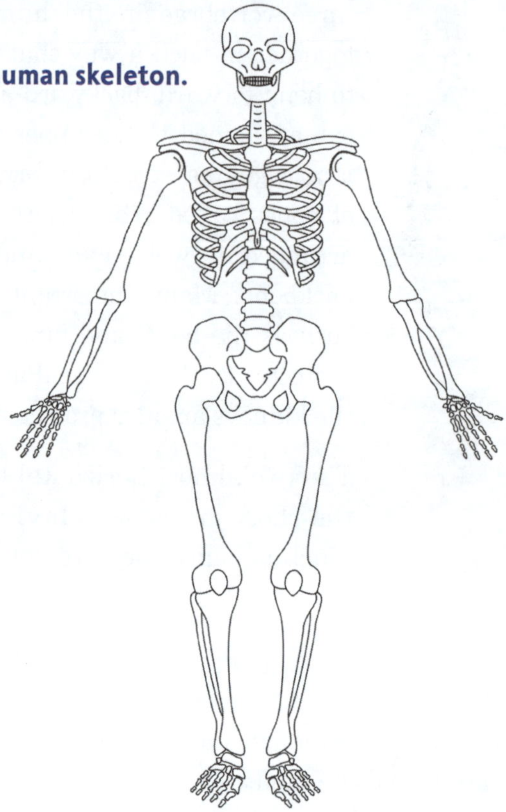

Joints

Although bones are rigid, the human skeleton is overall very flexible. There are many bones present in each part of the body, but the body can be bent only at those points where there are joints. Joints occur where two bones meet. The human body can perform more than one kind of motion because it has joints. These make the skeleton flexible and without them, movement would be impossible.

The main joints of the body—found at the hip, shoulders, elbows, knees, wrists and ankles—are freely movable. They are filled with a fluid, which acts as a lubricant to help the joints move easily.

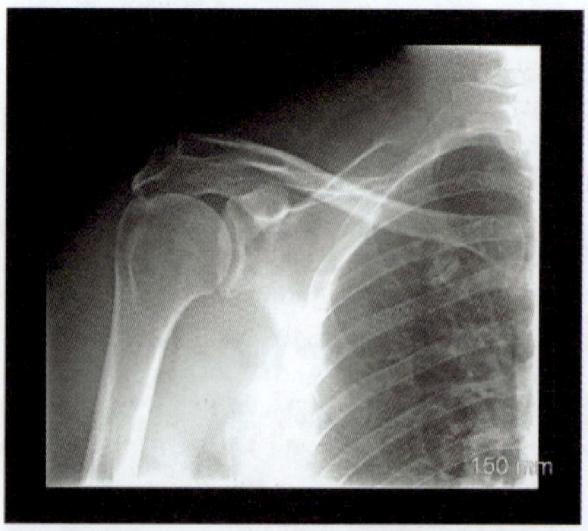

Ball-and-socket joint of the shoulder

Different types of joints in our body help us carry out different movements and activities.

1. The widest range of movements is provided by a **ball-and-socket joint**, in which the ball-shaped

head of one bone lodges in the hollow cavity of another. In the shoulder joint, the humerus fits into the socket of the shoulder blade and thus makes it the most mobile joint in the body. Here the socket is shallow and the joint loose. That is why the shoulder joint can easily get detached if pulled strongly.

The hip joint is also a ball-and-socket joint where the ball of the femur's head fits tightly into a deep socket in the hip bone. A rim of cartilage lining the socket helps grip the femur firmly.

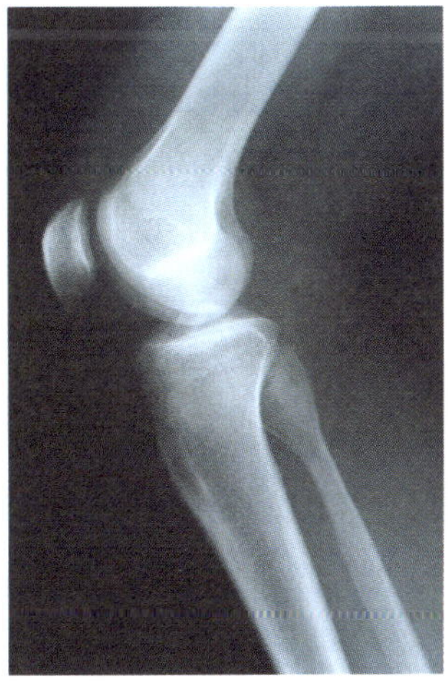

Hinge joint of the knee

2. A **hinge joint** allows movement only in one direction and permits the body parts to bend and straighten. It is found in the knees, elbows and the joints of the fingers and toes. The hinge joint of the knee is the body's largest joint and is unusual because it can swivel on its axis, allowing the foot to turn from side to side. However, it does not allow the leg to bend forward at the knee.

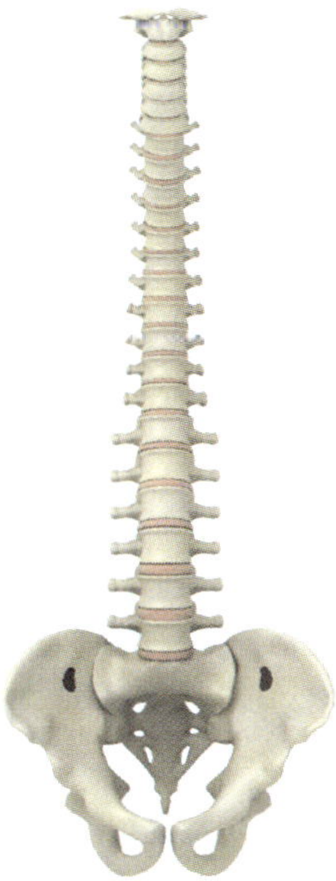

Gliding joints of the spine

3. A **gliding joint** allows bones to glide past each other. The ankles, wrists and spine on humans are gliding joints.

4. A **pivot joint** allows bones to spin and twist around other bones. Pivot joints allow rotation around an axis. There are pivot joints in the neck at the top of the spine, which allow the head to turn around, and in the smaller bone of the forearm, which allow the latter to twist.

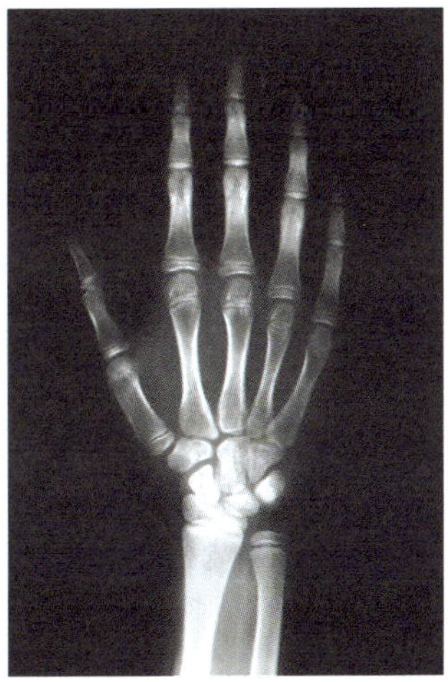

Saddle joint in the thumb

5. A **saddle joint** is more versatile than a hinge joint and a gliding joint since the bones can rock back and forth and from side to side. But they have limited rotation. The only saddle joints in the body are in the thumbs.

Factastic

When babies are born, their skull bones are not joined together yet. In fact, there are four pieces that do not join together until the baby is eighteen months old.

6. Apart from the joints mentioned above that allow movement, there is one type of joint that does not allow any movement at all and is known as a **fixed joint**. Such a joint is found between bones that do not move at all such as the joints in the skull.

Circle Time

Get into groups of four or five and make models of the different joints in the human body using wooden sticks, rubber or plastic balls, plastic or metal bowls, paper tubes and any other material you find suitable.

Using the models find out how each type of joint moves.

Besides bones, which are hard and inflexible, there are parts of the skeleton that are not as hard as bones and which can be bent. These are called **cartilage**. The nose and the upper part of our ears are made of cartilage, which hold their shape but can be easily flexed without breaking. Cartilage is also found at the ends of bones in some joints of the body. Here the cartilage acts as a shock absorber and reduces friction between the bones.

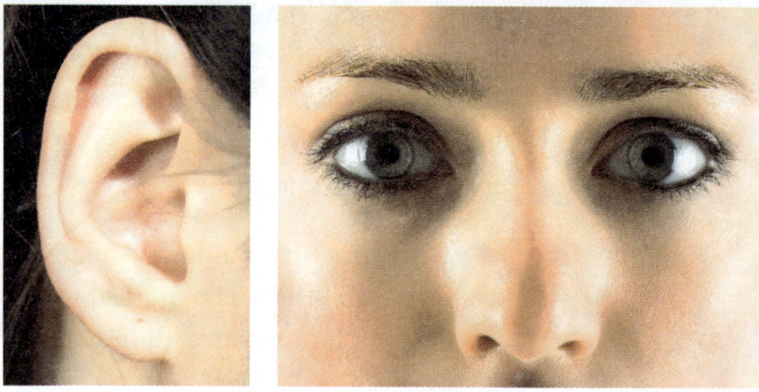

Cartilage in the ear and the nose

Muscles

The joints in the bones allow the human body to walk, bend, lift things and carry out many other activities. But the bones cannot move by themselves; **muscles** make them move. Movement is brought about mainly by the **contraction** (becoming smaller in length) of muscles. When contracted, the muscle becomes shorter, stiffer and thicker. It pulls the bone, making it move.

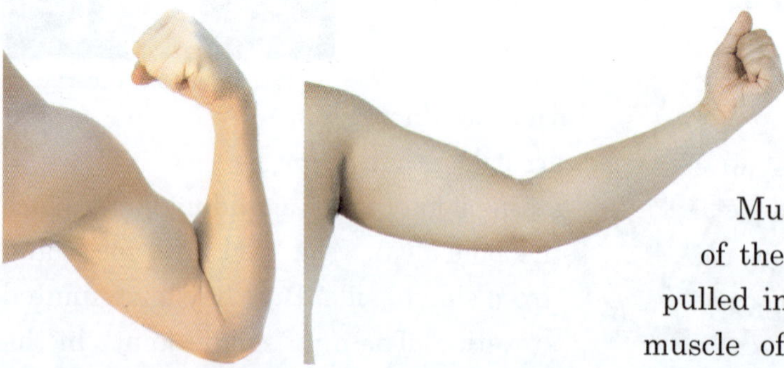

Flexed (contracted) and relaxed muscles

Muscles work in pairs. When one of the muscles contracts, the bone is pulled in that direction while the other muscle of the pair relaxes (lengthens). To make the bone move in the opposite direction, the relaxed muscle contracts to pull the bone towards its original position, while the first muscle relaxes. A muscle can only pull; it cannot push. Thus, two muscles have to work together to move a bone.

X-Rays

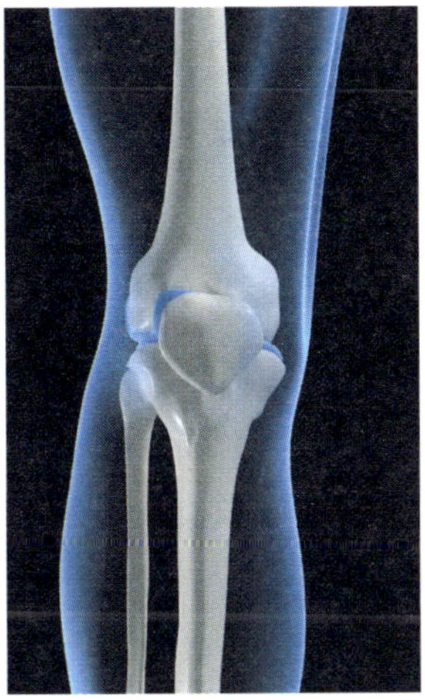

X-ray of human knee joint

In a living body, the shapes of the bones inside can be visualised to some extent by feeling them. But it is also possible to 'view' the bones in a living human body using invisible radiation known as X-rays.

X-rays are widely used in hospitals to make images of bones, especially to spot injuries such as fractures. The X-ray images show the bones as white shapes against a dark background. X-ray images are formed because X-rays cannot pass through bones, which are much denser than muscles and other soft tissues of the body. If a bone has a fracture it can be easily seen in the image, which helps the doctor to 'set' the fractured bone in the right way.

Animal movements

Unlike humans, most animals with backbones do not stand or walk upright; most walk on four legs. Birds and bats have the ability to fly while fish and whales can live and swim in water. Snakes use a movement which is similar to crawling. Invertebrates, such as earthworms, snails and insects, have their own unique movements and they have features designed to carry out their particular modes of movement.

The Earthworm

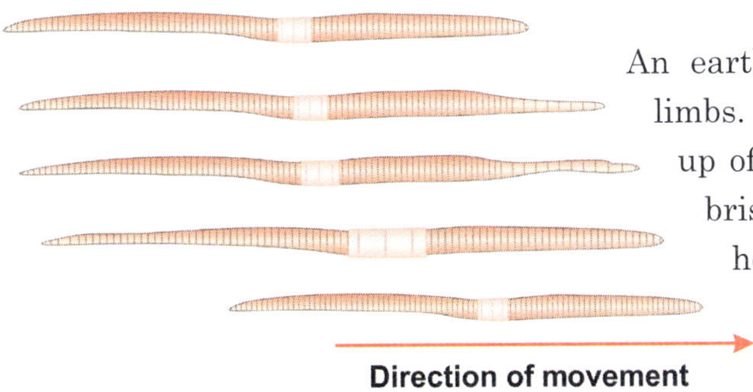

Earthworm movements

An earthworm does not have a skeleton or limbs. The body of an earthworm is made up of many rings joined end to end. It has bristles on each segment called **setae** that help the earthworm to move. It has two sets of muscles—one that makes it long and thin and one that makes it fat.

Earthworms move underground by means of waves of muscular contractions, which alternately shorten and lengthen the body. The earthworm first extends the front part of its body, keeping the rear portion fixed to the surrounding soil with its setae, which act as anchors. Then it fixes the front end while releasing the rear end. This makes it move forward by a small distance. Repeating such muscle expansions and contractions, the earthworm can move through soil. The earthworm's body secretes a slimy substance to help the movement.

The earthworm actually eats its way through the soil! Its body then throws away the undigested part of the material that it eats. This activity of an earthworm makes the soil more fertile and useful for plants.

The Snail

Snail

Snails can be found in gardens, in ponds and even in the sea. They belong to a group of animals with a soft body called molluscs, which are related to oysters, clams and other shellfish. They have soft, unsegmented bodies that are protected by a hard, round shell. This shell is known as the **exoskeleton** and is made of calcium carbonate. The shell is a single unit and does not help the snail in moving from place to place. It has to be dragged along.

A snail moves by creeping on a flat, thick structure at the base of its body that is made of a strong muscle. It is called its 'foot' underneath the body. The band of muscles in the foot contract and expand and this creates a kind of rippling movement that pushes the snail forward. The snail's foot has a special gland that produces slimy mucus to make a slippery track on which the snail can glide. Such silvery tracks can often be seen in the garden. The slime comes out from the front and hardens when it comes in contact with air. A snail is able to move on very sharp pointed needles, knives, razors and vines without being injured because the mucus-like secretion helps to protect its body.

The Cockroach

Cockroach

A cockroach is a typical insect that can walk and climb as well as fly in the air. It has three pairs of legs that help in walking. The body of a cockroach is protected by a hard covering called an exoskeleton. This outer skeleton is made of different units joined together that permit movement. There are two pairs of wings attached to the breast.

The breast muscles move the wings when the cockroach flies. Cockroaches also have muscles near the legs that are used to move the legs for walking.

Factastic

- Cockroaches have been around since the time of dinosaurs!
- A cockroach can live for almost a month without food and about two weeks without water.
- A cockroach can live for up to one week without its head!
- Cockroaches can hold their breath for up to 40 minutes!

The Fish

The body of a fish is so designed that it can move through water with minimum resistance. The body is typically fat in the middle and tapers at both ends, which makes it **streamlined**. Water can flow around a fish's streamlined body, allowing it to move fast in water.

Most fish have a bony skeleton in the middle covered with strong muscles. Fish swim by exerting force against the surrounding water. While swimming, muscles make the front part of the body curve to one side while the tail part swings towards the opposite side. Then, quickly, the body and tail change directions, thus imparting a wavy motion to the body and pushing it ahead. A series of such motions make the fish swim forward, helped by the fins of the tail. Fish also have other fins on their body, which mainly help to balance it. The fins also act as rudders helping the fish to swim in a particular direction.

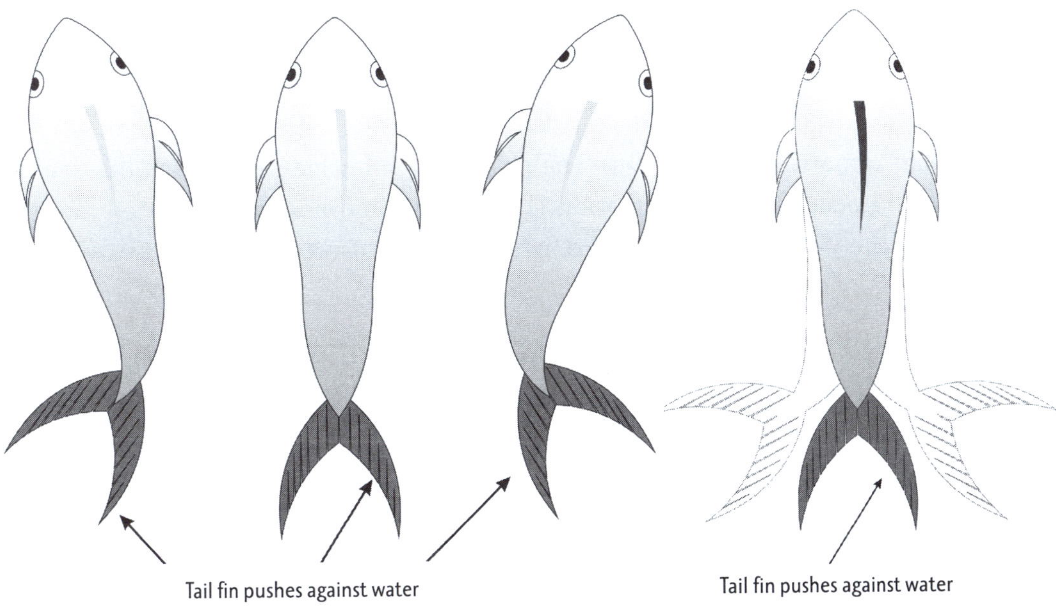

Movement of a fish

Apart from fish, mammals, such as dolphins and whales, also swim in the same manner.

The Snake

Snakes do not have arms or legs, but they have a long backbone and ribs. They also have many thin muscles and their body is covered with scales. Snakes use their bodies in a special way to move. Most snakes slither on the ground by alternately flexing their body to the left and to the right. This is called **lateral undulation**, which results in a series of backward-moving 'waves', making the body move forward. Snakes use this method for moving in water and on land.

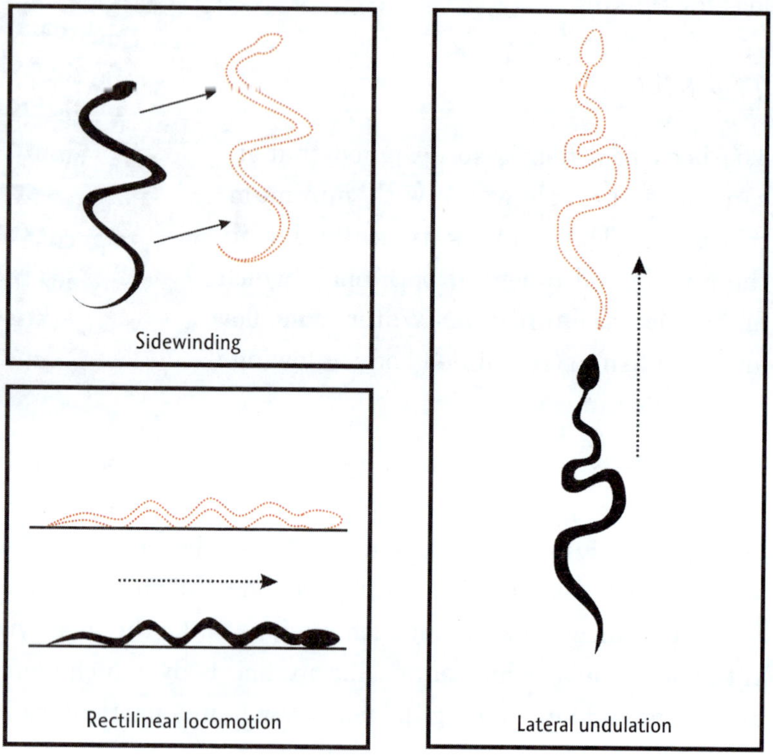

Movement of a snake

Some snakes use the method of **sidewinding** for moving. The body segments oriented in one direction remain in contact with the ground. While the other segments are lifted up, resulting in a peculiar 'rolling' motion. This method of movement is used mainly by snakes, such as the viper and rattlesnake, which live in deserts where there are no rocks or objects to push against.

Heavy snakes, such as pythons, boas and vipers, use **rectilinear locomotion**. They lift the scales and move forward by pulling the body along with the scales. This is the slowest method by which snakes move.

Circle Time

Form groups of five in class. Each group needs to collect a different small animal such as earthworms, snails, cockroaches, small fish, etc.

Each group should carefully observe how the animal moves and record their observations. Discuss what is common between the ways the different animals move.

Birds

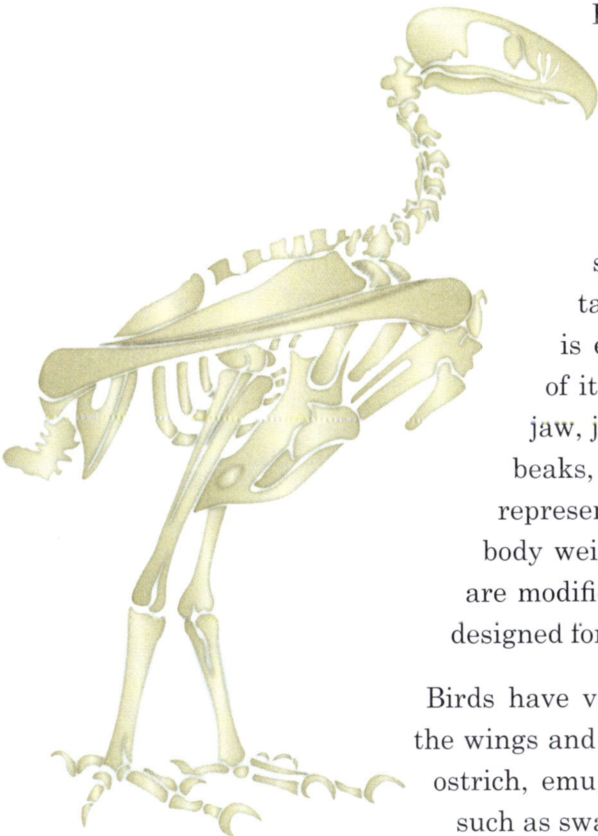

Skeleton of a bird

Birds are vertebrates. But their body structure has many unusual adaptations from other vertebrates, mostly to make flying easier. The bird skeleton is highly adapted and highly streamlined for flight. It is extremely lightweight but strong enough to withstand the stresses of taking off, flying and landing. A bird's skull is extremely light in proportion to the rest of its body due to the elimination of a heavy jaw, jaw muscles and teeth; instead birds have beaks, which are much lighter. The skull usually represents less than 1 per cent of a bird's total body weight. Birds have legs, but their forelimbs are modified into wings. The leg bones of birds are designed for walking and perching.

Birds have very powerful breast muscles that power the wings and help them fly. Certain birds, such as the ostrich, emu, kiwi and rhea, cannot fly, while some, such as swans, ducks and pelicans, have webbed feet that help them swim.

Factastic

The peregrine falcon (*Falco peregrinus*) is the fastest living creature, reaching speeds of up to 256 km per hour while diving from great heights to catch its prey.

Revision Time

* Bones play an important role in not only giving shape to the body but also along with muscles, help vertebrates in moving their limbs. They also protect the inner organs.
* The human skeleton is made up of a collection of bones of various sizes joined together in various ways to form the skull, the backbone, ribs, collarbone, hip bones and the bones of the hands and legs.
* Joints occur where two bones meet. The human body can perform more than one kind of motion because it has joints.
* Bone joints can be of many types, depending on the type of movement they allow.
* The bones at a joint are moved by alternate contractions and relaxations of two sets of muscles.
* Earthworms move through soil by the means of waves of muscular contractions that alternately shorten and lengthen its body.
* A snail moves by creeping on a flat, thick structure at the base of its body, which is made of a strong muscle. It is called its 'foot'.
* The body of a cockroach is protected by a hard covering called an exoskeleton. It has two pairs of wings for flying and three pairs of legs for walking.
* Fish swim by exerting force against the surrounding water by alternately curving the body and tail in one direction and then the other, thus imparting a wavy motion to the body and pushing it ahead.
* Most snakes slither on the ground by alternately flexing the body to the left and to the right.
* A bird's body is highly adapted and streamlined for flight. Birds have very powerful breast muscles that power the wings and help them fly.

Quiz Time

1. Answer the questions.

a. What are the various joints in the human body?

b. Where is the femur located in the human body?

c. Which is the only bone in the human skull that can move?

d. How is it possible to move the arm in all directions at the shoulder?

e. How are animals with soft bodies, such as snails, able to move from one place to another?

2. Fill in the blanks.

a. Animals without backbones are known as ________________.

b. The radius and the ulna make up the ________________ arm in humans.

c. Bones at the knee are joined by a ________________ joint.

d. The contraction of ________________ pulls the bones to cause movement.

e. Fish have a ________________ body that helps them in moving fast through water.

3. Indicate whether the statements are true or false.

a.	The cockroach has muscles near the legs.	True	False
b.	Most fish do not have bones.	True	False
c.	The tibia and fibula are bones of the upper arm.	True	False
d.	The human nose and the upper part of ears are made of cartilage.	True	False
e.	Movement at joints is brought about mainly by the relaxation of muscles.	True	False

4. Explain the terms.

a. mandible

b. saddle joint

c. cartilage

d. exoskeleton

e. streamlined

5. Project Work

The first column in the table below lists the different parts of the human body. Complete the second column indicating the type of joint present in the respective body parts.

Body part	Joint type
neck	
shoulder	

Body part	Joint type
elbow	
fingers	
wrist	
hips	
knee	
toe	
ankle	
thumb	
spine	

Think it over

1. **Why do people with arthritis find it painful to bend their arms and knees?**
2. **How can some snakes climb trees?**

10 Motion and Measurement

Things that we see around us are either moving or stationary. Many living things, such as birds, fish, insects, cows, dogs, lizards as well as people, move. Several non-living things can also move such as bicycles, cars, carousels, the hands of a clock, the wheels and needles of sewing machines, the blades of a fan and others. However, most non-living objects such as chairs, tables, houses, buildings, television sets, refrigerators, road hoardings and others, do not move.

Most non-living objects do not move

Sometimes an entire object may not move, but parts of it may. For example, a person may be standing or sitting in one place but moving his or her hand. A table fan may be stationary but its blades may be spinning. Whenever anything moves it changes its position.

Living things move

Types of motion

Motion can occur in various ways and can be classified as follows.

1. **Translatory motion:** The motion of an object that takes it from one place to another is termed as translatory motion. Objects that move can do so in two ways. If they move in a straight line—like sprinters in a 100-metre race, cars on a straight highway, a train on a straight track, or a stone falling from a height—the motion is called rectilinear motion. On the other hand, children riding on a merry-go-round, or a piece of stone tied to a string and whirled perform **circular motion**.

The translatory motion of a sprinter, a carousel and vehicles

Rotational motion of the earth and a top

2. **Rotational motion:** The earth moving on its axis or a top spinning on its tip are examples of rotational motion. Here the different parts of the object move at different distances at any given time. For example, the innermost part of the earth would move a lesser distance as compared to the surface of the earth.

3. **Periodic motion:** When an object repeats its motion after some time, the motion is called periodic **motion**. Common examples are a child on a swing, a branch of a tree moving to and fro in the wind, a swinging pendulum, and the needle of a sewing machine.

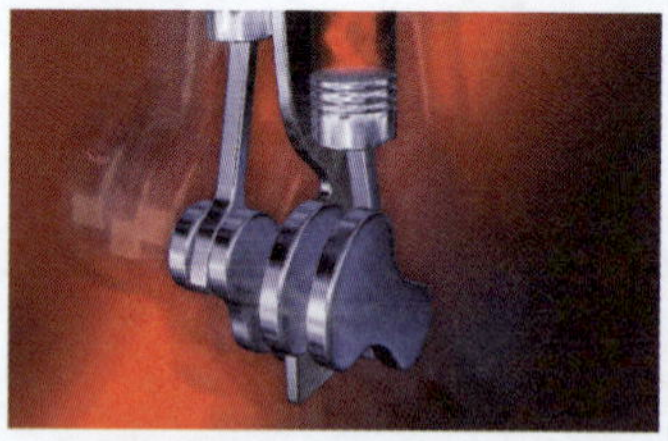

Periodic motion in a swing, a piston and a pendulum

rectilinear: in a straight line
periodic: happening at regular intervals

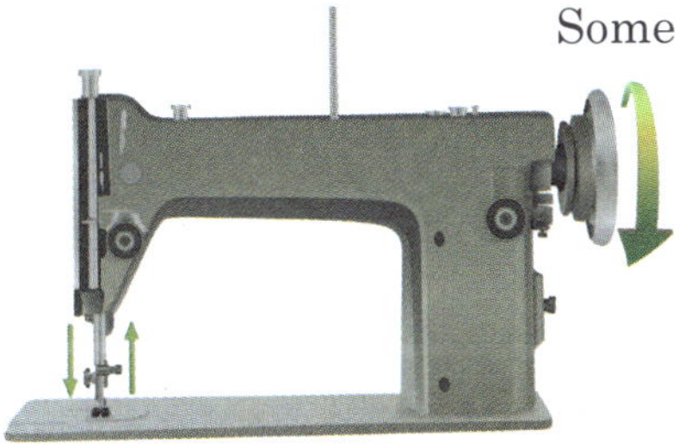

A sewing machine shows periodic and circular motion

Some objects may show more than one type of motion. For example, the wheel of a sewing machine shows circular motion, but the up-and-down movement of the needle shows periodic motion.

Explore

Find out from an encyclopaedia or the internet how an automobile works. Look at all the motions that come into play in a running car. This would include the motions of the pistons and the valves in the engine, the flywheel, the steering wheel, the wheels, the windscreen wipers, the brakes and so on.

Make a table showing the different kinds of motion involved.

When a bicycle is driven on a straight path, all points on the rim of the wheel perform circular motion, but the axles of the wheels and the bicycle as a whole move forward, performing rectilinear motion. When a screw is driven into wood by turning it with a screwdriver, it also performs two motions simultaneously—rotary or circular motion due to turning of the screw and rectilinear motion that makes it go into the wood.

Many kinds of transport

Bullock cart

All forms of transportation involve motion. Humans have been travelling since early days, only the modes of transport have changed over the years. Early humans walked on foot. Later, they rode on various animals to cover longer distances. The invention of the wheel brought about a great change and travelling

Camel-drawn cart

became much easier. Wheeled carts could be drawn by animals for travelling long distances. Horse-drawn carts and buggies, bullock carts as well as camel-drawn carts became popular.

Horse-drawn carriage

The beginning of the nineteenth century saw the invention of a new source of power—the steam engine. Railroads were made for steam engine-driven carriages and wagons to transport people and goods.

An aircraft

For travelling along water routes, boats have been used since ancient times. Initially, boats were built of reeds tied together with ropes and then with logs of wood. Later, people learnt to put together different pieces of wood and give shape to the boats. Sail boats allowed for long voyages along rivers. Steam power made it possible to build large ships that could carry thousands of passengers across the oceans.

An electric train

A ship

As technology advanced, better means of transport became available for moving from one place to another. The early years of the twentieth century saw the development of aeroplanes. Motor vehicles and aircrafts made travelling longer distances easier and faster. Instead of travelling from one city to another, one could travel from one continent to another across oceans. Later came modern-day electric trains, monorails, supersonic aeroplanes and spacecrafts that brought in a revolution in the way people travel. Today it is possible to travel to space in rockets.

Factastic

Globe riding or Zorbing is a sport in New Zealand where one can sit inside a giant inflatable balloon that is cushioned by a thick layer of air and roll down a big hill.

Measurements

Measurement plays an important role in our life. For example, a carpenter needs to measure the height and width of a cupboard he has to make to calculate how much wood he would need to make it. A farmer needs to know the length and breadth or the area of his land to calculate how much seed he can sow and how much water he would need for his crops. For making clothes, a tailor needs to take measurements of the body to calculate how much cloth would be required. Measurement of distances is also quite important to know how far or wide a particular thing is. You may need to know how far the hospital is from your house or what is the distance between Delhi and Chennai. Measurement basically involves the comparison of an unknown quantity with some known quantity. This known fixed quantity is called a unit. The unit of measurement can be anything; even a short piece of stick. For example, one can use a stick to measure the length of a desk. But unless we know the exact length of the stick, we will not know the length of the object that has been measured by it. Measurements can also be done using a length of string, which can be folded many times and marked in divisions of half, one-fourth, one-

A carpenter taking measurements

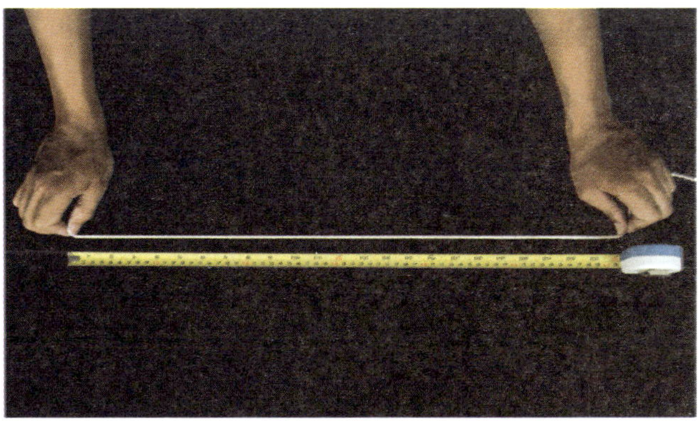

Measurement using string

eighth, etc. Any length to be measured, which is not a multiple of the full string length, can then be easily measured in terms of fractions of the 'string length', although this is not possible if a stick is used. But a stick or a piece of string as units of measurement cannot be used everywhere because the lengths of the stick or the piece of string are not standard units.

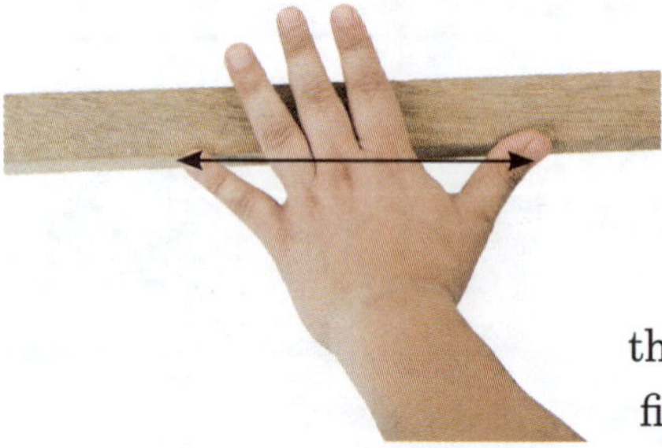

Span

In early days, people used units based on the dimensions of the human body for measuring length. They included units based on the distance between the tips of the stretched thumb and the little finger in an expanded palm, called a 'span'; or the length of the arm as measured from the elbow to the tip of the middle finger, called a 'cubit'; or the distance between the end of the outstretched arm and the chin, called a 'yard'. The human foot was no doubt the origin of the measuring unit called a 'foot' and was also for a long time the definition of its length.

Cubit

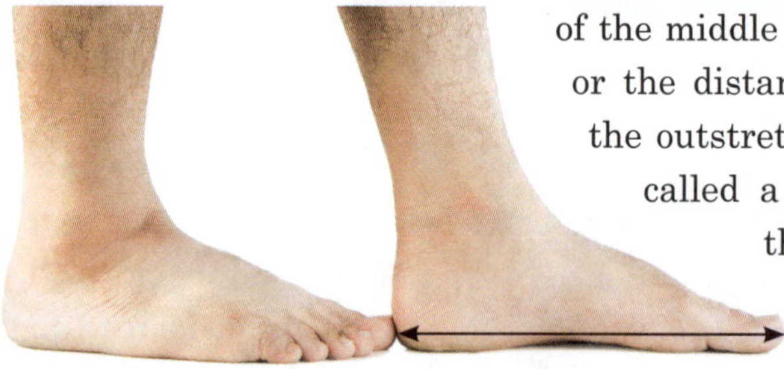

Foot

But, using dimensions of the human body as units of measurement has its own problems. Human beings differ widely in the size of their body parts. So the length measured using dimensions of the human body would differ from person to person, as would the measured length. Therefore, there was a need for units that were more accurate. Later, units of length, such as inch, foot, yard and mile, were defined by law and were used in many countries.

However, using these units had their own problems because each unit was a different multiple of another. For example, 12 inches made a foot; 3 feet made a yard; 1,760 yards made a mile and so on. To make things simpler, a standard system of measurement called the metric system was adopted in France in 1791 in which all the units were multiples or fractions of ten. The **International System of Units** (commonly known as SI units) is the modern form of the metric system and is the world's most widely used system of measurement, both in everyday commerce and in science. The SI unit of length is a metre, which is equal to 100 cm.

cubit: an ancient unit of length based on the length of the forearm
metric system: a decimal system of weights and measures based on the metre, kilogram and second

Fact File

Units of length

1 centimetre (cm)	10 millimetres (mm)
1 metre (m)	100 centimetres (cm)
1 kilometre (km)	1,000 metres (m)

Unit of Mass

1 gram (g)	1,000 milligram (mg)
1 kilogram (kg)	1,000 grams (g)
1 quintal	100 kilograms (kg)
1 metric ton	10 quintals

Accurate measurement of length

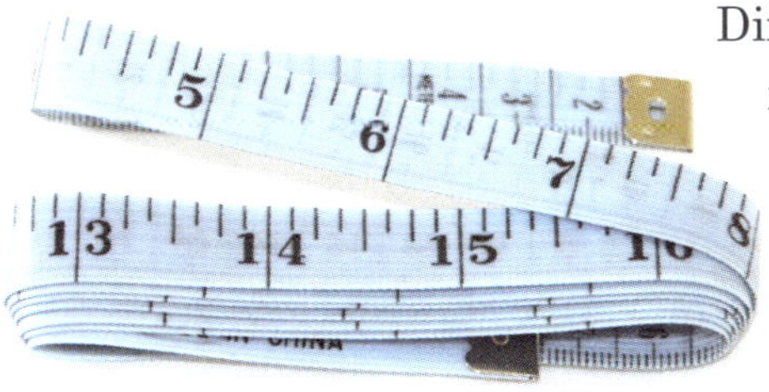

A measuring tape

Different types of measuring devices are used for measuring lengths or dimensions of different objects. For example, a metre-rod can be used to measure cloth or the length of a pipe, but it cannot be used to measure the girth of a tree or the size of one's chest. For such measurements, a measuring tape would be a better option. For small measurements, such as the length of a pencil or the size of a flower, a 15-cm scale normally found in a school geometry box would be enough.

A measuring scale

When taking any measurement, it is essential that the measuring scale used is accurate and the method of measuring is correct. For example, if a cloth merchant uses a metre-rod that is short by 1 mm, and the customer buys 10 m of cloth, he or she will receive 10 mm or 1 cm less cloth. For ensuring the correct usage of the measuring scale:

- The scale must be in contact with the object along its length.
- If the end of the scale is broken and the zero mark is not visible clearly, then it is better to avoid taking measurements from the zero mark. In such a case, the reading

may be taken from any other full digit on the scale and the value subtracted from the reading. For example, if the reading is taken taking 1 cm as the zero reading, then 1 cm has to be subtracted from the final reading taken. For example, if the final reading is 5.5 cm then the actual measured length would be 5.5 cm minus 1 cm; that is, 4.5 cm.

Factastic

Till 1960, the international standard metre was taken as the distance between two lines etched on a standard bar made of an alloy of 90% platinum and 10% iridium called the International Prototype Metre, measured at 0° C. But in 1960, the metre was redefined as equal to 1,650,763.73 wavelengths of light emitted by the krypton-86 isotope.

- The correct position of the eye is also important for accurate measurement, especially if the edge of the measuring scale is thick. The eye must be exactly in front of (or above) the point where the measurement is to be taken, otherwise, the reading may not be correct.

Measuring a curved line

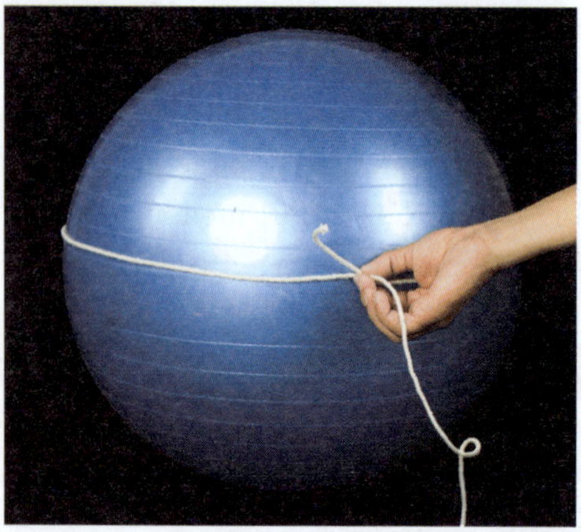

Measurement of curved length

The metre-scale and measuring tape are standard devices for measuring length or distance. But in some cases, an innovative approach is required, as for measuring the length of a curved line.

It is not possible to measure the length of a curved line directly by using a metre scale. The best way to measure it would be to use a thread. A mark can be made at one end of the thread by tying a knot or using a pen. After placing the mark at one end of the curved line, the thread can be laid carefully along the short lengths of the line till the other end of the curved line is reached, where another mark can be made on the thread. The distance between the two marks on the thread can then be measured using a standard metre scale to find out the length of the curved line.

Activity

Aim: Measure the distance that a paper aeroplane can travel.

Material required: a paper aeroplane, a measuring tape

Method: There are many ways of making a paper aeroplane. Check the internet and make three types of aeroplanes. Some could be pointed and while others may not. You need to test which aeroplane travels the furthest distance when thrown across the room. Throw each aeroplane about four times and then measure the average distance travelled using a measuring tape. Make a chart and record your observations.

	Aeroplane 1	Aeroplane 2	Aeroplane 3
Throw 1			
Throw 2			
Throw 3			
Throw 4			
Average distance			

Revision Time

- Things that we see around us are either moving or stationary.
- When a thing moves, it changes its position with time, and as long as it moves it is in motion.
- There can be three types of motion—translational, rotational and periodic.
- Some objects may show more than one type of motion.
- The measurement of lengths and distances plays an important role in our life.
- Measurement basically involves the comparison of an unknown quantity with some known quantity called a unit.
- In early days, people used units based on the dimensions of parts the human body such as span, foot, cubit, etc.
- In the metric system, all units are multiples or fractions of 10.
- The International System of Units (commonly known as SI units) is the modern form of the metric system and is the world's most widely used system of measurement, both in everyday commerce and in science.
- While measuring anything, it is essential that the measuring scale used is accurate and is used correctly.

Quiz Time

1. Answer the questions.

a. Why is the cubit not a good unit for measuring length?

b. What are the modern modes of transport and how do they differ from the ancient modes of transport?

c. What is rectilinear motion?

d. When a bicycle moves on a straight path, what kind of motion do the pedals perform?

e. Why is an elastic measuring tape not used to measure distances?

2. Fill in the blanks.

a. When a body moves in a straight line it is called ________________ motion.

b. A child on a swing performs ________________ motion.

c. Whenever anything moves it changes its ________________ with time.

d. In the metric system, all the units are multiples or fractions of ________________.

e. The metre is now defined as equal to a certain number of wavelengths of light emitted by an isotope of the element ________________.

3. Indicate whether the statements are true or false.

a.	A child on a merry-go-round performs periodic motion.	True	False
b.	The human foot can be used as a standard unit for measuring distance.	True	False
c.	A metre-scale cannot be used for measuring the length of a curved line.	True	False
d.	The correct placement of the eye is not important for taking measurement.	True	False
e.	The distance between the end of the outstretched arm and the chin is called a cubit.	True	False

4. Explain the terms.

a. periodic motion

b. SI units

c. rectilinear motion

d. circular motion

e. units of measurement

5. Project Work

a. Take a metre scale and a measuring tape. Ask your classmate to open his/her right palm fully and stretch the thumb and little finger. Measure the distance between the tip of the thumb and tip of the little finger, or the 'span', using the metre scale. Next, measure the length of his/her right foot, from the back of the ankle to the tip of the toe, with the metre scale and make a note of it. Next, with the measuring tape measure the distance between his/her right elbow and the tip of the middle finger of his/her right hand and record the measured length of the 'cubit'. Repeat the same with as many classmates as possible and record your observations in the table given below.

Name of student	Span (cm)	Foot (cm)	Cubit (cm)

Are the lengths of the 'span', 'foot', and 'cubit', as measured for each student, the same? Do you think units of measurement based on dimensions of the human body are useful for measuring distances?

b. Measure the width of the teacher's table in your classroom in terms of your hand span. Record the width as the number of full spans and the number of 'finger widths' in case it is smaller or larger than a certain number of full spans. After measuring the width of the table with your hand, again measure the width with a metre scale. Let all the other students measure the width of the table in a similar way and record the observations in the table given on the next page:

Name of student	Size of desk (in spans and fingers)	Size of desk (in cm)

Study the values obtained by different students very carefully. The values in the column that has the measurement done using hands will be different.

Think it over

In which part of a car engine is periodic motion converted into circular motion?

11 Light, Shadows and Reflections

Light is a form of energy and travels freely in space. We cannot see anything when there is complete darkness and need light to see objects. Light carries information from the things around us to our eyes and brain. There are some objects that produce and emit light such as the sun, stars, candles, kerosene lanterns, tungsten bulbs, CFL tubes, LED torches, neon signs and even fireflies. Such objects that give off light of their own are known as **luminous** objects and they can be seen directly. We can see various other objects around us only because light falls on them and they are illuminated by some luminous source. If there is no luminous source around, nothing would be visible.

Luminous objects: firefly, CFL bulb, neon sign, LED lights

During the day, the sun is the brightest source of light that illuminates half of our planet. But at night, we can only see the moon and stars in the sky. The moon, the planets and comets can be seen in the night

CFL: compact fluorescent lamp
LED. light emitting diode

sky because the sun reflects off these heavenly bodies. Without sunlight these would not be visible. Moon light is actually the light of the sun reflected from the surface of the moon.

> **Factastic**
> Light moves at a speed of 3,00,000km per second.

Light travels in a straight line. Although we cannot feel it, but light travels at a definite speed, which is very high. The sun is almost 150 million kilometres away from the earth. However, light from the sun takes only a little more than 8 minutes to reach the earth.

Non-luminous objects: moon and planets

Transparent, opaque and translucent materials

When light falls on an object, four things can happen: (i) the object may allow the light to pass through; (ii) it may totally block the light; (iii) it may allow a part of the light to pass through; or (iv) it may reflect the light. Materials, such as glass, clear plastic, water and air, allow light to pass through making it possible to see through them. Such materials are called transparent. Window glass is transparent and allows light to come in and allows people inside to have a view of the outside. All spectacle lenses are made from transparent materials so that the wearer can see through them. Transparent glass or plastic containers make the contents inside clearly visible, as do glass panes of display cabinets. In contrast to

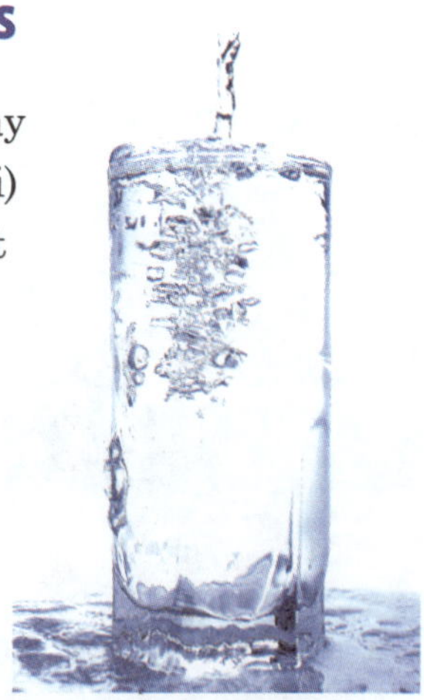

Transparent object

> **transparent:** material that allows all light to pass through

Opaque object

transparent materials, some materials block all light falling on them and do not allow any light to pass through. They are called opaque materials. Bricks, concrete, wood, cardboard, metal sheets and cement asbestos sheets are examples of opaque objects. It is not possible to see through an opaque material and hence objects kept inside a metal or wooden box or in a closed room cannot be seen from the outside. Some materials are neither totally transparent nor totally opaque. They allow some light to pass through. Such materials are called translucent. Fibreglass roofs, frosted glass and fine bone china are materials that allow some light to pass through but do not allow a clear view of objects on the other side. Factories often have roofs made of corrugated fibreglass sheets to allow daylight to filter through. This helps to cut costs of lighting.

Explore

Collect different kinds of material—sheets of glass, polythene, rubber, metal, tracing paper and writing paper, pieces of different kinds of plastic, broken pieces of crockery, cardboard, flower petal, brick, tile, etc. Hold each object in front of your eyes and look at a source of light. Depending on what you see—whether you can see the light source clearly, or see it hazily or cannot see it all—group the objects as transparent, translucent and opaque, respectively.

Shadows

When light falls on an opaque object, it cannot pass through. Such an object will block the light and hence a dark area will appear behind the object, which is known as its shadow. Since light travels in a straight line, the shape of a shadow usually resembles the shape of the object forming it.

opaque: material that does not allow light to pass through
translucent: material that allows some light to pass through
fibreglass: a covering material made of glass fibres in resins
frosted: having a roughened coating resembling frost
shadow: an area of shade with clear boundaries

A shadow of a child

Shadows of trees

The shape of the shadow of an opaque object would also depend on how the object is oriented with respect to the source of light and the surface on which the shadow is formed. For example, the shadow of a CD would appear to be circular, elliptical or like a straight line, depending on how it is held in front of the light source.

Shadows of CDs

Explore

Some people can fold their hands in such a way that their shadows form shapes of animals. How many shapes can you form with your fingers. Draw them on a piece of paper.

Many natural phenomena, such as eclipses, are nothing but the formation of shadows. A solar eclipse takes place when the moon comes in between the sun and the earth in a straight line and the shadow of the moon falls on earth. Similarly, a lunar eclipse takes place when the earth comes between the sun and the moon in a straight line and the shadow of the earth falls on the moon.

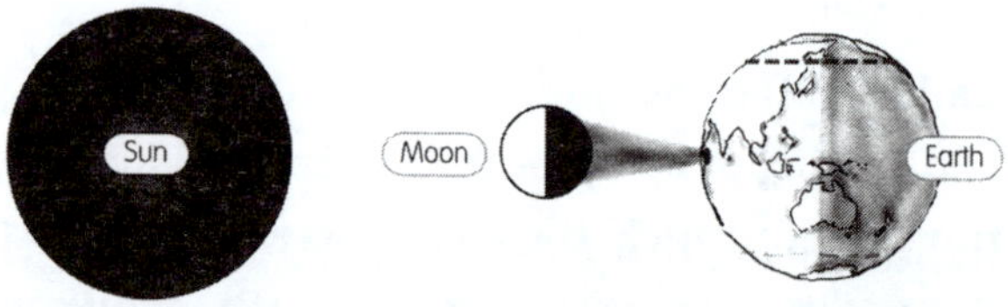

Solar eclipse

Lunar eclipse

But a shadow can form only on a surface, such as the ground, a wall or a screen. If there is no surface that is available on which the shadow can fall, then a shadow will not form. A shadow cannot form in air. A shadow shows only the outline and not the details. The size of a shadow varies depending on the distance between the object and the source of light and the distance between the object and the screen on which the shadow is cast.

Factastic

From the round shape of the shadow of the earth falling on the moon, the early Greeks had correctly guessed that the shape of the earth was spherical.

Explore

Take a cube-shaped box. Stand outdoors in the sun and hold the box in your hand so that it casts a shadow on a white card placed on the ground. Turn the box in different ways and see how the shape of the shadow changes. Which of the following shapes do you see in the shadows as you turn the box: square, rectangle, hexagon, octagon, pentagon, rhombus? Why does the shape of the shadow change as you turn the box?

Colour of shadows

It is usually believed that the colour of a shadow is always black. But, this is not true. Shadows can be coloured too. However, the colour of a shadow does not depend on the colour of the object casting the shadow. Normally, since bright sunlight is white light, shadows appear black. But, if light of any other colour is used, the colour of the shadow will be different. The colour of a shadow will usually be the **complementary colour** of the light falling on the object, especially if the light source is large. Complementary colours are any two colours that are directly opposite each other, such as red and green or yellow and blue. These opposing colours create maximum contrast when used together. Since black is the complementary colour of white, the colour of a shadow formed by white light appears black. Similarly, if red light is used, the colour of the shadow will be green.

Pinhole camera

Light casts a shadow when it strikes an opaque object because it travels in a straight line. This property is used to make a simple device called the 'pinhole camera', which is in the shape of a closed box. At one end is a pinhole through which light travelling in a straight line creates an image of the outside scene on the opposite end of the box. If a tracing paper is fixed

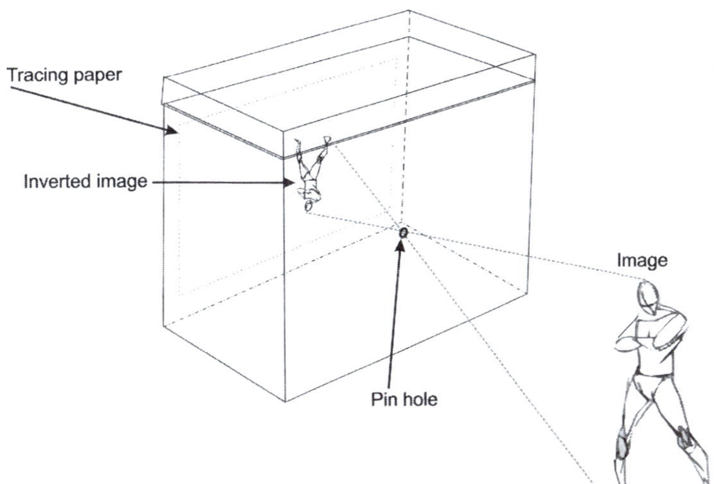

Pinhole camera

pinhole camera: a closed box with a pinhole at one end

at the opposite end, the image formed can be seen. If a photographic film is placed at the end where the image is formed, photographs of brightly lit objects or scenes can be taken. The image formed by a pinhole camera is inverted. This happens because light travels in a straight line. When light from the top of an object passes into the camera through the pinhole, it goes straight to the bottom of the screen at the back of the camera. Similarly when light from the bottom of the image passes through the pinhole, it goes straight to the top of the screen. This forms an inverted image of the object.

Pinhole images can be seen in nature also. When the sun is high in the sky, small circular patches of light can be seen under large trees. The small circles of light are actually images of the sun formed by the sun rays passing through tiny spaces between the dense leaves of the tree, which act as pinholes.

Reflection

Light waves follow the law of reflection. Light always travels in straight lines. It appears to bend while reflecting. Reflection is light bouncing off a very smooth surface. The path of a light beam reflected from the surface of a plane mirror forms an angle. The light can be reflected in almost any direction, depending on the angle at which the plane mirror is held.

Image formed by a plane mirror

Explore

Make a pinhole camera from a cardboard box that has one end open. Cut out a square hole, about 1 cm across, at the end that is opposite the open end of the box and cover this end with aluminium foil. Prick a tiny hole through the aluminium foil for light to enter the box. Cover the open end with a piece of tracing paper.

Hold the pinhole camera in a dark room, pointing the tiny hole at the view outside an open window. Make sure that the objects you wish to look at through your pinhole camera are in bright light. Do you see an image on the tracing paper screen?

mirror: polished surface, usually a glass plate with coating of silver or aluminium that forms images by reflecting light

Mirrors are common in households, shops and commercial establishments. By looking into the mirror we can see our own face or objects in front of it as reflection on the other side of the mirror. But the image that we see in a plane mirror is not real; it is called a **virtual image**.

The most common type of mirror is the plane mirror, which has a flat surface and produces an image that is almost identical to the object. But curved mirrors also exist that produce magnified or smaller images or simply distort the reflected image. 'Funny mirrors', often seen in science museums, have curved surfaces that make the viewer look funny by distorting the face and body shapes.

Funny mirror

Activity

Aim: To see the illusion of a bent ruler.

Material required: a ruler and a glass of water

Method: Take a glass that is half filled with water. Place a ruler in it and look at it from the side of the glass. What do you see? When we see the ruler from the side of the glass, light plays tricks on our eyes and the ruler looks bent.

Conclusion: The ruler appears bent because light travels slower through water than through air. As the light enters the glass of water, it slows down (changes direction) and as it leaves the glass it moves fast again. Hence, the ruler looks as if it is bent.

Plane mirrors can be used to bend light around corners. Normally, it is not possible to see what is on the other side of a brick wall. But a periscope is a device that makes it possible to see things that lie on the other side of a brick wall. By using two plane mirrors fixed at a 45° angle at the two ends of a long tube as shown, a periscope can be built that makes it possible to see what is on the other side of a wall or any other opaque obstacle.

periscope: an optical instrument that provides a view of an otherwise obstructed field

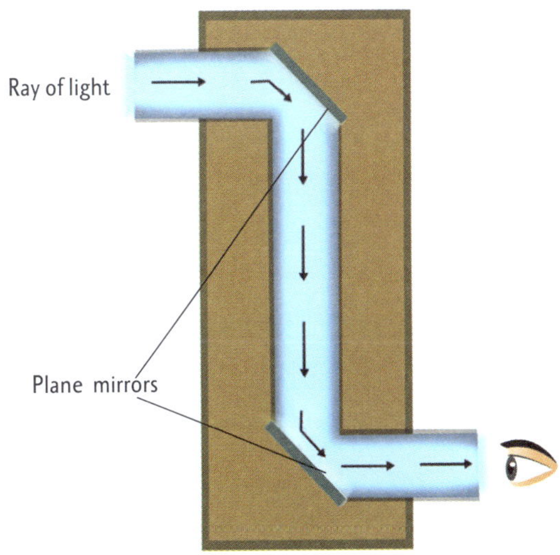

Periscope

Circle Time

Invite a few of your friends to your terrace or an open ground at night. Get an LED torch and a plane mirror. Ask one of your friends to stand on your right at some distance and hold the mirror. Ask the other friends to stand in a semicircle around you. Switch on the LED torch and shine the beam onto the mirror held by the friend on your right so that the beam is reflected back to you.

Can you make the light beam fall on each of your friends standing in a semi-circle turn by turn without moving the torch? What does this activity prove? Discuss.

Activity

Aim: To create a mirror drawing to observe lateral inversion.

Material required: **a hardboard, a pencil and a mirror**

Method: **Keep the hardboard inclined in such a way that you can see it in the mirror. The mirror and hardboard should face each other. Now keeping your eyes on the mirror, draw a picture of the alphabet 'P' on the hardboard. Then, look the picture that you have drawn. What does it look like?**

Conclusion: ____

Revision Time

* We cannot see in complete darkness; we need light to see objects.
* Objects that give off light of their own are known as luminous objects and they can be seen directly.
* Materials can be of three types—transparent, opaque and translucent.
* Materials that allow light to pass through making it possible to see through them are called transparent.
* Materials that block all light falling on them and do not allow any light to pass through are called opaque.
* Some materials that are neither totally transparent nor totally opaque and allow some light to pass through are called translucent.
* A shadow is an area where direct light from a light source cannot reach due to obstruction by an object.
* Many natural phenomena, such as eclipses, are nothing but the formation of shadows.
* The colour of a shadow is complementary to the colour of the light falling on it.
* Normally, light travels in a straight line, but if it is made to fall on the surface of a mirror, it gets reflected by the mirror.
* Plane mirrors can be used to reflect light around corners.

Quiz Time

1. Answer the questions.

a. If there were no sun, why would the moon be invisible?

b. What are materials that block all the light falling on them called?

c. What will be the colour of a shadow formed by the light of yellow colour?

d. Why is the image formed by a pinhole camera inverted?

e. How can plane mirrors be used to deflect light around a corner?

2. Fill in the blanks.

a. An LED torch, a CFL bulb, neon signs, a candle flame are all ____________________ objects.

b. We can see the moon, the planets and comets in the night sky because the ____________ ____________ lights them up.

c. Materials that allow light to pass through are called ____________________.

d. The colour of a shadow usually will be the ____________________ colour of the light falling on it.

e. The image formed by a plane mirror is a ____________________ image.

3. Indicate whether the statements are true or false.

a. The moon and the planets are luminous objects.	True	False
b. Materials that allow all light falling on them to pass through are called translucent.	True	False
c. The shape of shadows is always like the objects forming them.	True	False
d. A shadow can form only on a surface.	True	False
e. Complementary colours create least contrast when used together.	True	False

4. Explain the terms.

a. luminous

b. transparent

c. reflection

d. pinhole camera

e. virtual image

5. Project Work

Think of as many luminous objects as possible. Use an encyclopaedia or the internet to find out how they produce light. In the first column in the table below, enter the names of the luminous objects and in the second column, against each item, describe briefly how it produces light.

Luminous object	How it produces light
LED torch	
sun	
tungsten bulb	
candle	
CFL bulb	
neon tube	
fire crackers	
firefly	
kerosene lamp	
gas light	

Think it over

1. **Why does a plane or a bird not cast a shadow on the ground?**
2. **Why is the image formed in a pinhole camera not as sharp as an image created using a lens?**

12 Electricity and Electric Circuits

Electricity is a form of energy that is used to provide heat, light, power, etc. This energy is fueled by the transfer of electrons from positive and negative terminals within a conductor. The SI unit of the electrical force is **volt**, commonly called voltage. The voltage between two points is the electrical force that would drive an electric current between those points.

The use of electricity in our daily life today is so prominent. Electric lights, electric fans, air conditioners, electric pumps, refrigerators, electric trains, metro trains, traffic signals, televisions, music systems, computers, telephones, mobiles, to name a few, cannot work without electricity. Factories cannot run nor can offices work without electricity.

Learn More

Make a list of all the appliances that you use in a single day that require the use of electricity.

Electricity transmission lines

Most electricity consumed is generated by power stations using coal, gas, radioactive material, such as uranium, or the force of water. Electricity generated at power stations is carried to smaller substations at high voltage through transmission lines and from there sent to homes at low voltage through overhead or underground cables. In India, electricity is supplied to homes at 220–230 volts, which is rather dangerous for people if not used carefully. If someone accidentally comes in contact with a 220-volt current, it may cause serious injury or death. The electricity generated by portable generators is equally dangerous. Children should never handle electric gadgets without adult supervision.

Dry cell

Dry cell

For most school activities that need the use of electricity, dry cells, commonly known as batteries, are the best. A dry cell produces current at low voltage. Dry cells do not have any liquid in them and hence can be handled safely. They are easily available and are used in a wide variety of gadgets such as LED or bulb torches, transistor sets, alarm clocks, digital cameras, tape recorders and many others.

All cells that produce electricity have two terminals; a positive terminal (+) and a negative (–) terminal. A dry cell has a small metal cap at one end, which is the positive terminal, and a metal disc at the other, which is the negative terminal. Dry cells come in many sizes, but all of them produce electricity at the same voltage, that is, about 1.5 volts. If a higher voltage is required, many cells can be joined together in series. For example, by joining six dry cells, one can get electricity of $6 \times 1.5 = 9$ volts.

Factastic

Dry cells can be of two types: primary and secondary. Primary cells can be used only once and when one stops working, it has to be replaced by a new one. Secondary cells on the other hand, can be recharged by connecting to a 220-volt electric supply and can be used over and over again.

Fact file

When a dry cell is connected to a device, such as a bulb, through a switch and the switch is turned on, a limited amount of current flows through the circuit, depending on the resistance of the bulb. But if the two terminals of the cell are joined directly, without connecting them with a switch and a bulb or some other device, a short circuit is caused. As a result, a large amount of current flows through the circuit for a short time and the cell stops working because chemicals in the cell get used up very fast. Sometimes, a short circuit may cause a fire also.

terminal: a contact on an electrical device (such as a battery) through which electric current enters or leaves
switch: a mechanical or electrical device for making or breaking connections in a circuit
circuit: an electrical device that provides a path for electrical current to flow
resistance: a material's opposition to the flow of electric current

A dry cell produces electricity as a result of chemical reactions. As the cell is used, the chemicals stored inside are used up and electricity production becomes reduced. That is why after extended use, a torch gives only dim light since the bulb does not get enough voltage. When the chemicals are used up, the cell stops producing electricity and has to be replaced with a new one.

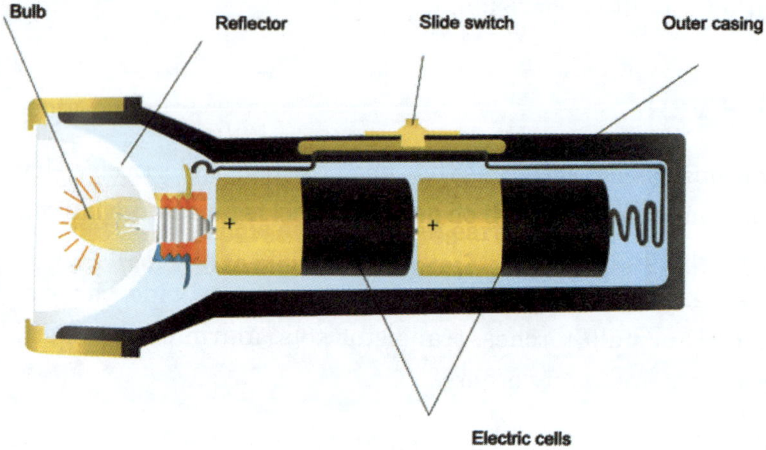

Cross section of a torch

A battery-powered torch has a bulb that lights up when the switch is moved to the 'on' position. The bulb used in a torch is similar to a light bulb used in homes but is much smaller in size. It consists of a small glass envelope, which contains a thin filament made of tungsten. This filament glows bright and gives off light when current is passed through it. The filament is supported by two thick wires that carry current to the filament when the torch is switched on. One of thick wires is connected to the outer case of the bulb, which forms the base and is usually made of brass. The other thick wire is connected to a raised metal point visible in the middle of the base. The outer brass case and the central metal point at the bottom are the two terminals of the bulb. These two terminals are fixed in such a way that they do not touch each other. When connected to a battery, they carry current to the filament to light the bulb.

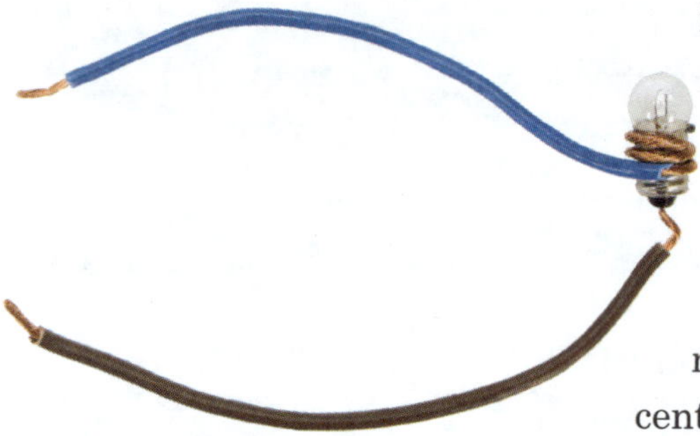

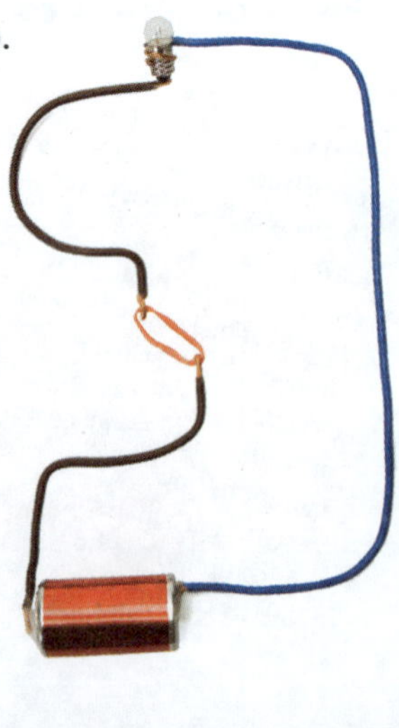

As long as the filament remains intact, the bulb glows and produces light. But sometimes the filament burns up or breaks and the bulb does not produce any light. At such times, the bulb is said to be 'fused' and has to be replaced.

filament: a thin wire in an electric bulb that is heated white hot by the passage of an electric current
tungsten: a metallic element that melts at a very high temperature

Activity

Aim: To find out, how a torch bulb is lighted up by a dry cell.

Material required: electrical wires, a bulb, a dry cell, rubber bands and electrician's tape

Method: Attach two wires to the two terminals of the bulb using either the electrician's tape or by soldering it to the central metal tip at the base of the bulb. Connect the free ends of the two wires that have been fixed to the torch bulb (labelled A and B) to the two terminals of the dry cell using rubber bands in the following ways.

1. A to the positive terminal and B to the negative terminal.
2. B to the positive terminal and A to the negative terminal.
3. Both A and B to the positive terminal and a free wire to the negative terminal.
4. A to the positive terminal and leave B free. Attach a piece of free wire to the negative terminal.
5. A to the positive terminal and B to the piece of free wire attached to the negative terminal.

Note down in which of the cases the bulb lights up.

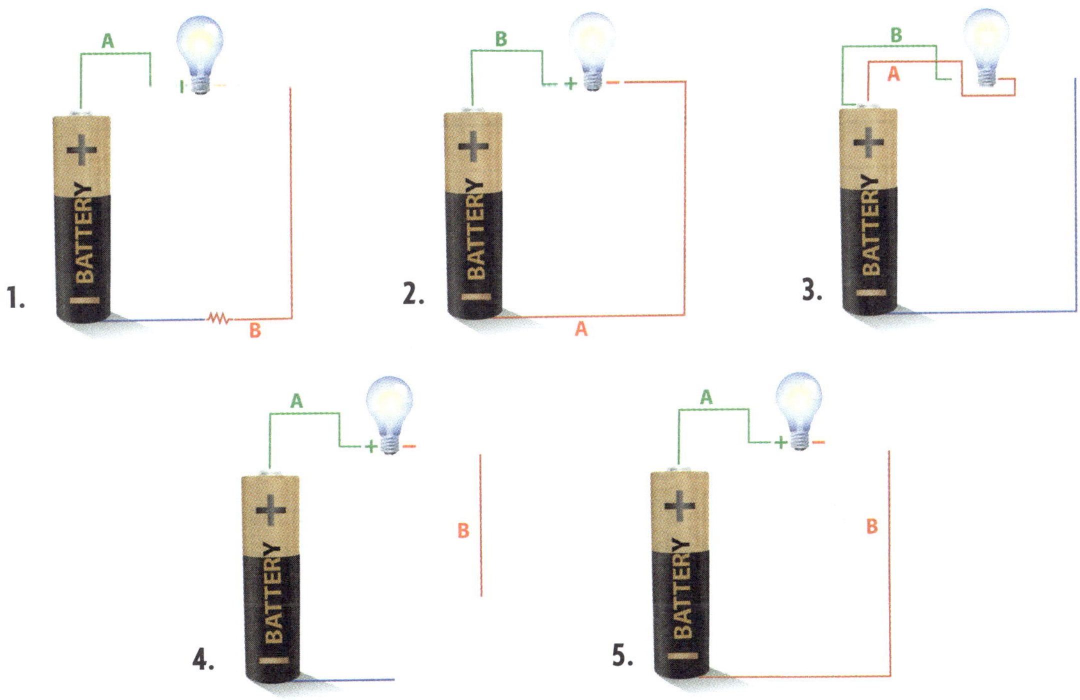

Can you explain why the bulb lights up only in a few cases?

Learn More

The bulb in a battery-powered torch lights up when the switch is pushed. From the outside it is difficult to see how it works. It can be better understood by making a simple model.

Take a torch bulb, a dry cell and a piece of wire. Remove the plastic covering at the two ends of the wire so that the metal part is exposed. Wrap one end of the wire around the base of the torch bulb. Fix the other end of the wire to the bottom (negative) terminal of a dry cell with a rubber band.

What happens when you bring the tip of the base of the bulb in contact with the top (positive) terminal of the cell? What happens if you move the bulb away from the top terminal of the cell?

Electric circuits

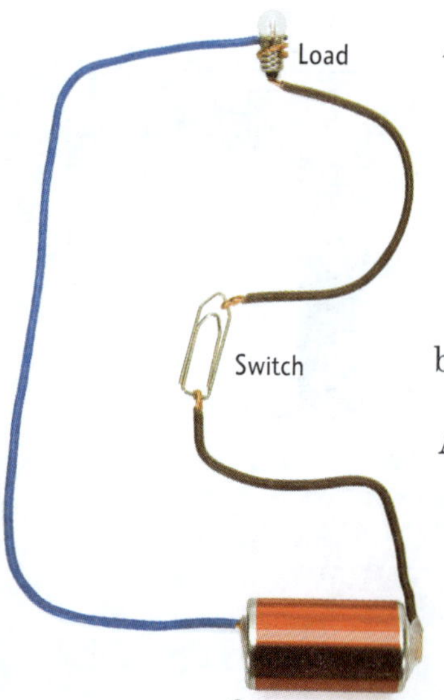

A torch bulb lights up only when the two wires attached to the bulb are attached to two separate terminals of the dry cell because only then can current flow from the cell through the filament. Such an arrangement is an example of an electric circuit that provides a complete path for the electric current to flow between the two terminals of the dry cell. The bulb lights up only when current flows through the circuit.

An electric current is nothing but the flow of electrons from the negative terminal to the positive terminal of the dry cell. But in an electric circuit, the direction of current is taken to be from the positive to the negative terminal of the battery.

Electric switch

Any electric circuit is incomplete without a switch, which is a device to connect and disconnect the source of electricity (the battery) to the load (the torch bulb). Without a switch, current will flow continuously through the circuit, even when it is not needed. At

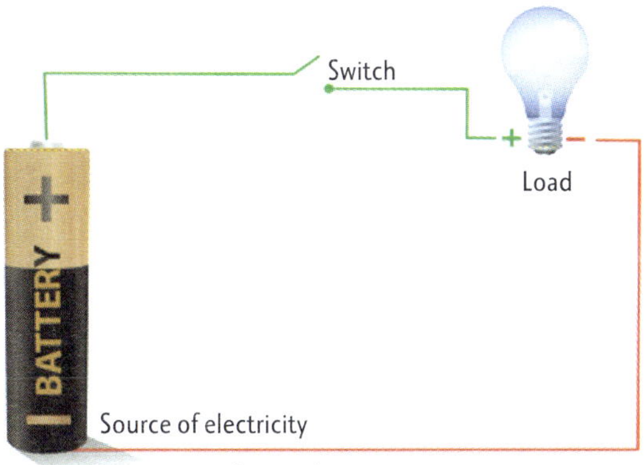

Incomplete circuit

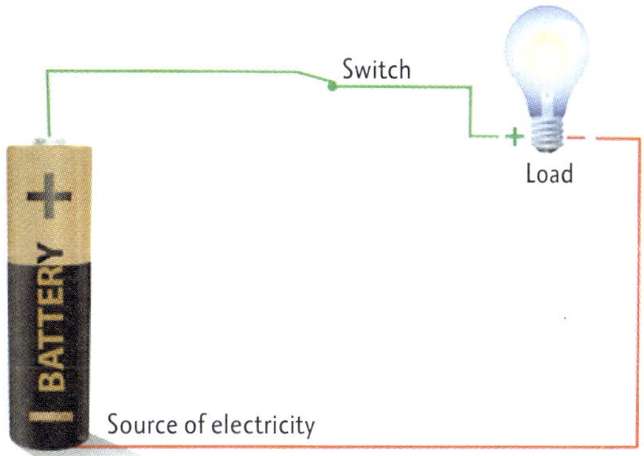

Complete circuit

home, all electrical appliances, such as lights, fans, air conditioners, etc., have switches that can be used to turn the appliances on and off. Even in a battery-powered torch, a switch is used to connect the battery to or disconnect it from the bulb.

Activity

Aim: To make a simple switch.

Material required: a piece of wood, drawing pins, pieces of wire, clip, a dry cell and a bulb

Method: Insert one drawing pin into the loop at the end of one clip and fix it on the piece of wood. Make sure that the clip is free to rotate around the pin. Then, fix the other drawing pin on the same piece of wood a little distance away from the first one so that the free end of the clip can touch it when rotated. Attach the two ends of a wire to the two board pins. The switch is ready. When the free end of the clip is away from the second drawing pin, the switch is in the 'off' position and when it touches the second drawing pin, it is in the 'on' position.

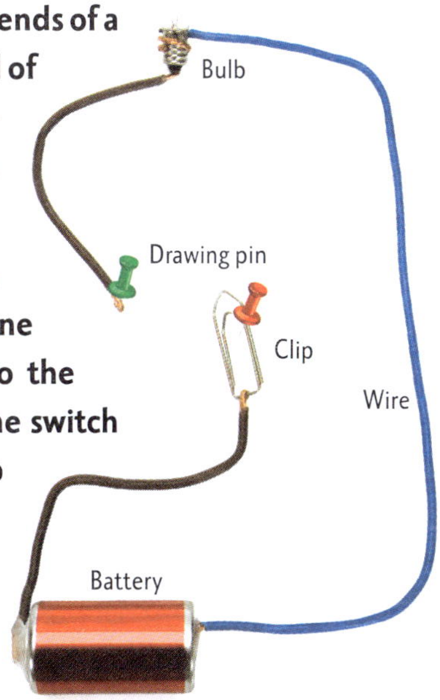

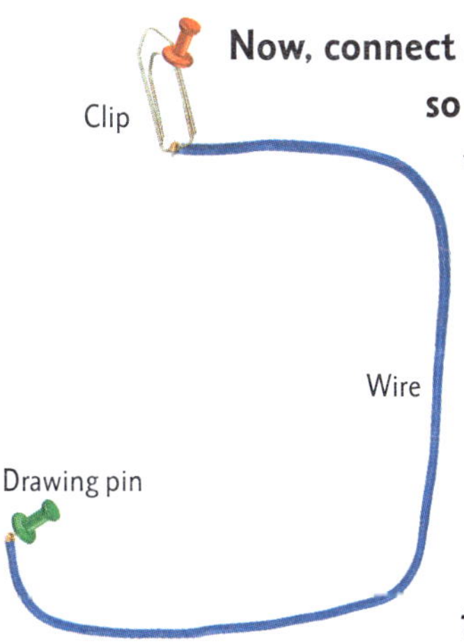

Now, connect a dry cell and a bulb with this switch so that one terminal of the battery and one wire from the bulb are connected to the wires attached to the two ends of the switch and the other wire from the bulb is directly connected to the other terminal of the battery. Observe what happens when the switch is off or on. When does the bulb light up? Do all switches work in the same way?

Conductors and insulators

A substance or medium that conducts or allows an electric charge to flow through is known as a **conductor**.

> **Factastic**
> Among the metals, silver is the best conductor of electricity, but copper is most commonly used in electrical wire applications because of its low price. Gold does not conduct electricity very well, but is used in electrical contacts because it does not corrode easily.

Usually copper wires are used for making electrical circuits because electric current can flow easily through copper. Hence, copper can be said to be a good conductor of electricity. Most metals are good conductors of electricity. But there are also materials that do not allow electric current to pass through. Such materials are called **insulators**. Insulators, such as rubber and plastics, are used for covering electrical wires, plug tops, switches and other parts of electrical appliances that are commonly used at home. Before using a copper wire in an electrical circuit, the insulating layer on the ends must be removed; otherwise no current will flow through the circuit.

Good conductors are easy to distinguish from insulators by the way electric current passes through them. If a conductor is part of an electrical circuit then current can flow easily and if a bulb is connected in the circuit, it will light up. On the other hand, if an insulator is connected in the circuit, no current will flow and the bulb will not light up.

Activity

Aim: To observe how a fluorescent tubelight lights up without connecting it with wires to an electric circuit.

Material required: a fluorescent tubelight and a piece of polythene

Method: Take a fluorescent tubelight to a dark room. Take a piece of polythene and rub it vigourously along the tubelight.

Conclusion: The static electricity that is produced causes the tubelight to glow.

Revision Time

- ✶ Electricity is generated at power stations or obtained from dry cells.
- ✶ A dry cell produces electricity during a chemical reaction.
- ✶ Dry cells can be of two types–primary and secondary.
- ✶ Primary cells can be used only once, but secondary cells can be recharged and used over and over again.
- ✶ All cells that produce electricity have two terminals—a positive terminal and a negative terminal.
- ✶ An electric bulb has a thin tungsten filament sealed inside a glass envelope that glows, giving off light when current is passed through it.
- ✶ An electric circuit provides a complete path for the electric current to pass.
- ✶ A switch is a simple device that is used to either break an electric circuit or to complete it.
- ✶ Materials that allow electric current to pass through them are called conductors.
- ✶ Materials that do not allow electric current to pass through them are called insulators.

Quiz Time

1. Answer the questions.

a. What is an electrical circuit?

b. Mention the uses of a dry cell.

c. What is a short circuit?

d. Where are insulators used?

e. What is the purpose of an electric switch?

2. Fill in the blanks.

a. In India, electricity is supplied to homes at ____________ volts.

b. A dry cell generates electricity from ____________ reaction.

c. A ____________ cell can be recharged and used over and over again.

d. Materials that allow electric current to pass through are called ____________.

e. As long as the ____________ remains intact, a bulb will glow and produce light.

3. Indicate whether the statements are true or false.

a. Electricity generated at power stations is carried to substations at low voltage through transmission lines. True False

b. If the two terminals of a dry cell are connected directly, it causes a short circuit. True False

c. Secondary cells can be used only once. True False

d. The filament of a torch bulb is made of steel wire. True False

e. In a dry cell, electric current flows from the negative terminal to the positive terminal. True False

4. Explain the terms.

a. generator

b. filament

c. circuit

d. conductor

e. insulator

5. Project Work

The first column in the table has a list of objects. In the second column, write down the name of the material each item/object is made of. In the third column, write down whether the material is a conductor or an insulator on the basis of whether it makes the bulb in the tester light up or not.

Object	Material it is made of	Conductor/Insulator
eraser	rubber	insulator
nail	iron	conductor
paper		
plastic cup		
pencil		
candle		
glass plate		
coin		
spoon		
knife		

From the table do you find anything common between the materials that are good conductors of electricity? Which materials do you think are good conductors and which are bad conductors? Can you tell why?

Think it over

1. **Why are metals good conductors of electricity? Why are most non-metals not good conductors?**
2. **Why is it not possible to recharge a primary cell?**

13 Understanding Magnets

A magnet is an object that has the capacity to attract certain metals, such as iron, nickel and cobalt. It can also attract or repel another magnet. Magnets are used to make several appliances that are used in our daily life. Pin holders, fasteners of handbags, cupboard doors, telephones, fans, doorbells, refrigerators, washing machines, music systems, radio, TV, tape recorders, CD and DVD players, computers, juicer grinders, cars, electric motors, generators and ATM machines are just a few of them. A very common application of magnets is to stick things onto the refrigerator. Since the outer shell of most refrigerators is made of metal, a magnet will readily stick to it. Magnets are also used in industry for a variety of purposes, especially for moving heavy pieces of iron junk. The earth itself behaves like a huge magnet and hence a magnetic needle points in the north–south direction because of the earth's magnetic field.

Explore

Look around and list gadgets and appliances that use magnets. Look up reference books or the internet and find out where magnets are utilised in each of these appliances. Do you find some common pattern in the use of magnets in these appliances? For what purpose is a magnet used in most appliances?

Discovery of magnets

repel: cause to move back by force
magnetic field: an area around a magnet within which its attraction is felt

There are many legends about the discovery of magnets. One of the most common is that of an elderly shepherd named Magnes, who was herding his sheep in an area of northern Greece called Magnesia, some 4,000 years ago. It is said that the nails in his shoes and the metal tip of his stick happened to get firmly stuck to the large, black rock on which he was standing. This type of a rock that contained iron was subsequently named **magnetite**. People soon realised that magnetite not only attracted objects made of iron, but when a small piece of it was suspended in mid air, it always pointed to the north–south direction creating a primitive compass. This led to an alternative name for magnetite, that of lodestone or 'leading stone'.

Factastic

Many scientists believe that birds are able to find their way home by using the earth's magnetic field to guide them on long-distance flights during their yearly migration.

Poles of a magnet

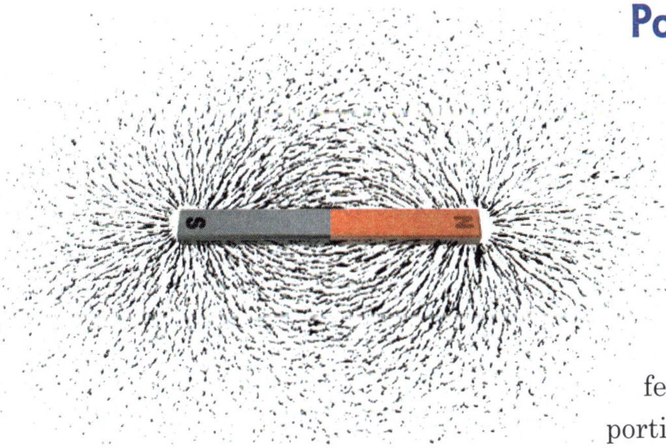

North pole and south pole of a magnet

Every magnet has two 'poles' at its two ends where the force of attraction is the strongest. If iron filings (fine particles of iron) are sprinkled over a bar magnet, most of the filings stick to the two ends of the bar with very few particles sticking to the middle portion. If a bar magnet is suspended freely on a string, it will come to rest in a north–south direction and the same pole of the magnet will always swing toward the north. Therefore, it is called the north-seeking pole or simply the **north pole** of the magnet. The other pole of the magnet is the south-seeking pole or the **south pole**.

It is not possible to have a magnet with only one pole. If a bar magnet is broken into half, each of the broken pieces will also have two poles. If the smaller pieces are further divided into still smaller pieces, each of the smaller pieces will also have two poles.

Activity

Aim: To show the direction in which a magnet points.

Material required: **a bar magnet, a piece of string, a piece of paper, a wooden ruler and an iron nail**

Method: Take a bar magnet and tie it in the middle with a thread. Suspend the magnet with the thread from a stand so that it is just a little above a sheet of paper placed below the stand. Leave the magnet free to rotate and let it come to rest. Mark two points on the sheet of paper to show the position of the ends of the magnet. Draw a line joining the two points.

Without moving the stand and the sheet of paper, lightly turn the magnet again and let it come to rest. Again, mark the two points showing the positions of the ends of the magnet. Turn the magnet in different directions and note its position when it comes to rest.

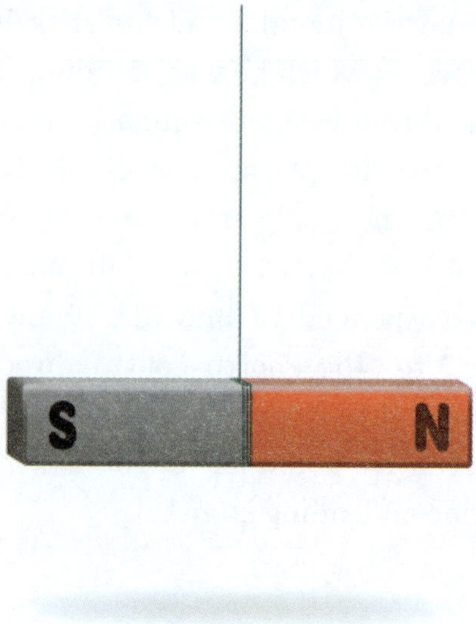

A bar magnet suspended in air always points in the north–south direction

Does the magnet always come to rest pointing in the same direction? From the direction in which the sun rises in your locality, find out the north and south directions. Using this you can figure out which end of the magnet points to the north and which points to the south. Mark the two ends of the bar magnet as N and S, meaning 'north seeking' or north pole and 'south seeking' or south pole.

Repeat this activity with a large iron nail and rulers made of wood and plastic. Do these materials also always come to rest pointing in the same direction? Can you tell why only a magnet points in the north–south direction?

Conclusion: ____________________

Making a magnet

There are many ways of making magnets from pieces of iron or steel. The simplest method is to rub a piece of iron with a strong magnet repeatedly. A piece of steel rod can also be turned into a magnet by winding a coil of wire around it and passing electric current through the coil for some time.

Activity

Aim: To turn an iron nail into a magnet.

Material required: an iron nail, a bar magnet and iron filings

Method: Take an iron nail and rub it over and over in the same direction with the same end or pole of the bar magnet. Lift the magnet up each time your stroke gets to the end of the nail and start again at the same place with each new stroke. Do this about fifty times.

Next, take the nail near a few pins or some iron filings and see what happens. Does the nail attract the pins and iron filings? If you tie a string around this nail and suspend it from a stand, does it point in the north–south direction when it stops rotating? Does the nail behave like a magnet?

Conclusion: ______________________________

The **magnetic compass** that is usually used to find direction, is a device based on this property of magnets. A compass is usually a small round-shaped box with a glass cover on it. A magnetised needle is set on a pin in such a way that it can turn freely inside the box. The compass also has a dial with directions marked on it.

To find a particular direction, the compass is placed on a horizontal surface and the needle is allowed to come to rest, which it does in the north-south direction. The compass is then rotated until the north and south marked on the dial coincide with the respective ends of the needle. The other directions can then be easily found out from the directions marked on the compass dial.

Activity

Aim: To make a magnetic compass and show its working.

Material required: a bowl, a needle, a bar magnet and a cork

Method: Take a plastic bowl half filled with water, a medium-sized needle, a bar magnet, and a cork or a small piece of thermocol. Magnetise the needle by rubbing it with one end of the bar magnet, as described earlier.

Next, push the needle through the cork evenly so that the needle projects equally on both sides. Place the needle with the cork in the water-filled bowl. Make sure that the needle does not touch the water. If it does, take out the needle and push it into the cork at a higher level. The floating needle should now point in a north-south direction.

Rotate the cork, with the needle fixed in it. Note the direction in which the needle points when the cork stops rotating. Does the needle always point in the same direction when the cork stops rotating? Is this how a magnetic compass works?

magnetised: having the properties of a magnet

Attraction and repulsion between magnets

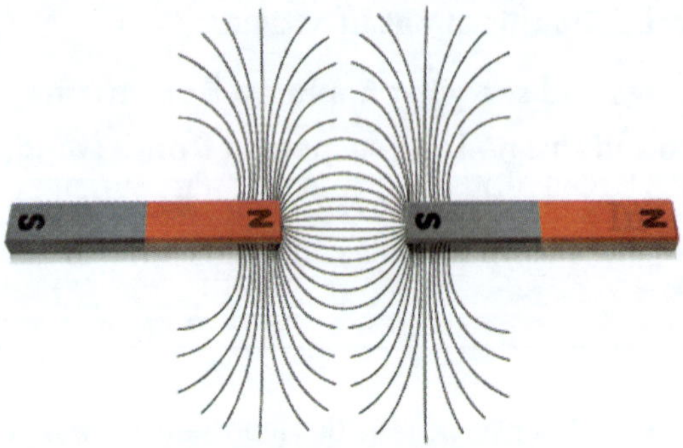

Attraction between magnets

One of the important properties of magnets is that unlike poles attract while like poles repel each other. A magnet attracts objects made of magnetic materials. But if two magnets are brought together whether they attract or repel each other would depend on which poles are facing each other. If opposite poles of two magnets are in proximity, they would strongly attract each other. But if similar poles of two magnets are brought together, they would strongly repel each other.

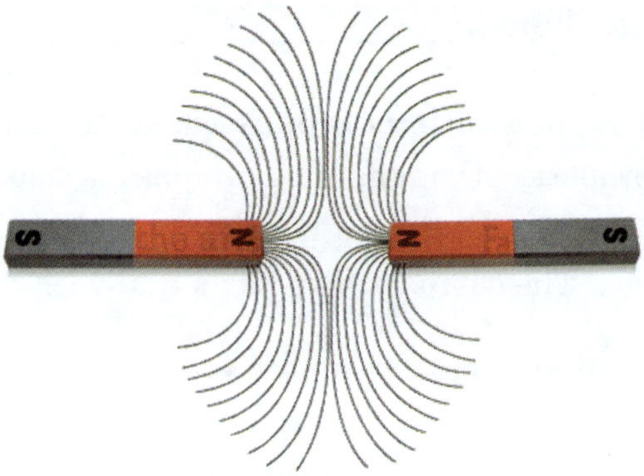

Repulsion between magnets

Activity

Aim: To study the nature of magnets.

Material required: two bar magnets

Method: Take two bar magnets. Find out their north and south poles by suspending them with a thread and noting the directions their ends point to when they stop rotating. Mark the two ends as N and S. Next, place the two magnets with their pole marked N and S on a smooth and dry surface, such as a flat glass or laminate surface, so that they can slide freely.

Now, move the magnets following the directions given below:

1. **Move the N-end of one magnet slowly towards the S-end of the other magnet.**
2. **Move the S-end of one magnet towards the N-end of the other magnet.**
3. **Move the N-end of one magnet towards the N-end of the other magnet.**
4. **Move the S-end of one magnet towards the S-end of the other magnet.**

In which of the four situations did the magnets attract each other? In which situation did they repel each other? Can you tell why?

Conclusion: ____________________

Types of magnets

Magnets can either be permanent or temporary.

Types of magnets

A **permanent magnet** is made from a material that is magnetised and retains its magnetism. An everyday example is the strip magnet that tightly holds the refrigerator door to the refrigerator body. Alloys, such as alnico (an alloy of aluminium, nickel, iron, cobalt) as well as ferrites (ceramic like materials made of iron oxides with nickel and cobalt), make excellent permanent magnets. Permanent magnets come in many shapes and sizes. Some examples of permanent magnets are bar magnets, horseshoe magnets, ring magnets and cylindrical or disc magnets.

A **temporary magnet** is one which acts like a magnet only when it is near a strong magnet and loses its magnetic property when the influence of the strong magnet is removed. **Electromagnets** are examples of temporary magnets. When electric current is passed through a coil wound around a steel rod, the steel rod behaves like a magnet. however, as soon as the electric current is stopped, the steel rod stops behaving like a magnet.

Often an electromagnet is wrapped around a core of iron, which increases the strength of the electromagnet. Electromagnets are used when really strong magnets are required such as in electrical appliances including electric motors, television sets, telephones, computers and many other modern devices.

Factastic

Recent trains called Maglev trains do not run on wheels. They use electromagnets to lift them off the ground so that they float on the rails. Floating reduces friction and allows the train to run more efficiently.

alloy: a mixture containing two or more metallic elements combined together

Magnetic and non-magnetic materials

A magnet attracts only objects made of certain materials

such as iron, steel, cobalt and nickel. However, objects made of metals, such as brass, aluminium, copper, gold, silver and stainless steel, as well as from materials such as plastic, rubber, glass and wood, are not attracted by a magnet. Materials that are attracted towards a magnet are called **magnetic** while those that are not attracted towards a magnet are called **non-magnetic**. Only magnetic materials can be turned into magnets.

Explore

Take a horseshoe magnet and bring it near different objects one by one. Make a list of those objects that are attracted towards the magnet and those that are not. How many objects do you find are magnetic and how many are non-magnetic?

Keeping magnets safely

Magnets lose their magnetic properties if they are heated, hammered or dropped from a height. Also, magnets become weak and lose their strength if they are not stored properly. To store them safely, bar magnets should be kept in pairs with their unlike poles on the same side with two pieces of soft iron placed across their ends. A horse-shoe magnet can be stored safely by keeping a piece of iron across the poles.

Magnets losing their magnetic property

All types of magnets should be kept away from magnetic media such as floppy discs, cassette tapes, credit cards, computer monitors, television sets and hand-wound watches.

Strong magnets

Activity

Aim: To check if our regular breakfast cereal contains iron and minerals.

Material required: **cereal, plastic bag, rolling pin and a strong magnet**

Method: **Put some cereal in a plastic bag, and close it. Place it on a table. Use a rolling pin to crush the cereal into powder. Now open the plastic bag and touch the magnet to the powder. Does the cereal cling to the magnet?**

Conclusion: ______________________________

Revision Time

* A magnet is an object that attracts certain metals such as iron, nickel and cobalt.
* The oldest known magnet is a black rock called magnetite found in Magnesia in northern Greece, 4,000 years ago.
* When made into the shape of a needle and freely suspended with a thread, a magnet always points in the north-south direction.
* Every magnet has two 'poles' at its two ends where the force of attraction is the strongest.
* The pole pointing north is called the north-seeking pole or simply the north pole of the magnet; the other pole is known as the south-seeking pole or the south pole.
* A magnetic compass is used to find direction.
* The unlike poles of magnets attract each other while like poles repel each other.
* A permanent magnet is made from a material that is magnetised and retains its magnetism.
* An electromagnet, which is a temporary magnet, is created when electric current is passed through a wire coiled around a steel rod. It ceases to act like a magnet after the current is turned off.
* Materials that are attracted towards a magnet are called magnetic materials while those that are not attracted towards a magnet are called non-magnetic materials.

Quiz Time

1. Answer the questions

a. Why does a bar magnet point in the north–south direction if suspended by a thread?

b. Where are the poles of a horseshoe magnet located?

c. If a bar magnet is broken into two pieces, how many poles will each of the broken pieces have?

d. What is a magnetic compass used for?

e. What happens when like poles of two magnets are brought together?

2. Fill in the blanks.

a. A magnet is an object that ________________ certain metals such as iron, cobalt and nickel.

b. At the two poles of a magnet, the force of attraction is ________________.

c. The south pole of a magnet would strongly ________________ the south pole of another magnet.

d. It is not possible to have a magnet with only one ________________.

e. An electromagnet stops being a magnet when the ________________ stops.

3. Indicate whether the statements are true or false.

a.	The earth behaves like a huge magnet.	True	False
b.	If a bar magnet is broken into half, each of the broken pieces will also have two poles.	True	False
c.	Electromagnets are used when strong magnets are not required.	True	False
d.	A magnet attracts only objects made of non-magnetic material.	True	False
e.	Magnets lose their magnetic properties if they are heated or dropped from a height.	True	False

4. Explain the terms.

a. magnetite

b. magnetic pole

c. permanent magnet

d. electromagnet

e. magnetic material

5. **Project Work**

Take a horse-shoe magnet or a bar magnet and bring it near different objects you see around. Enter the names of the objects in Column 1, as shown in the table given below. Mention whether the object is attracted by the magnet or not in Column 2. Based on observations made in Column 2, mention in Column 3 whether the object is magnetic or non-magnetic.

Object	Attracted/Not attracted	Magnetic/Non-magnetic
stainless steel spoon	not attracted	non-magnetic
iron nail		
brass plate		
aluminium foil		
refrigerator body		
glass bottle		
soft drink can		
door key		
one-rupee coin		

Do you find anything in common between the objects that are attracted by the magnet? What is common between them?

Think it over

1. **Why is it dangerous to take a magnet near a credit or debit card?**
2. **What would happen if a strong magnet is brought near a TV picture tube?**

14 All About Water

Water is the key to life on earth and without water all life including plants, animals and microbes would perish. Water makes up about seventy per cent of our body, and a large part of the food we eat. Clean water is colourless, odourless and tasteless and can dissolve many things.

Human beings use water for a variety of purposes—drinking, cooking, cleaning utensils, cleaning floors, washing clothes, bathing, gardening and several other activities. Since people do not use water wisely, a lot of water is wasted or gets polluted. This is another reason why there is a scarcity of water in several cities of the world. Most of the naturally occurring water is in the oceans and seas and cannot be used directly by humans since it has a high salt content. Water is also frozen in glaciers and polar ice caps and hence unavailable. Important sources of fresh water are groundwater, rivers and lakes.

Uses of water: Cooking, gardening, drinking, washing

Factastic

At present, an average person in India consumes only about one-tenth of the amount of water consumed per year compared to a person living in the United States or Europe.

polluted: rendered unwholesome and unfit for consumption by contaminants

Circle Time

Ask your friends to make a list of daily activities in which water is used. Ask them to measure the amount of water used for each activity by each member of their family during the whole day. They may use a glass, a mug, a bucket or any other container of known volume to measure the amount of water used. Discuss and come up with ways of reducing the usage of water in some homes.

Water for irrigation

Factastic

To grow 1kg of maize, about 600 litres of water are required; which is roughly equivalent to 30 large-sized buckets full of water. To produce 1kg of wheat, about 720 litres of water are required; and to produce one kilogram of paddy rice, 1,550 litres of water is required.

The amount of water that is used in any household is only a small part of the total water that is needed to meet many other requirements of our life. For example, water is needed in agriculture for growing food, and in industries for producing almost all the things of daily use.

Sources of water

It is known that almost two-thirds of the earth's surface is covered with water, but that water is salty and cannot be used for drinking, household purposes, growing crops or in industry. Yet, oceans play an important role in supplying the water that we use.

View of oceans on the earth

In homes, people get water from different sources depending on where they live. In cities and big towns, water is supplied through pipelines and is available from taps in homes. Tap water is usually drawn from

Ocean

a lake, a river or a deep tube well and is supplied through a network of pipes after the process of filtering and chemical treatment to remove germs.

People in villages get water mostly from rivers, lakes, wells and hand pumps.

Water cycle

Well

When water is left exposed to air, it disappears over time. For example, if water is spilled on the floor, it dries up after some time. Water from wet clothes disappears when left exposed to the air, making the clothes dry. What actually happens is that water slowly turns into vapour and mixes with the air. Evaporation of water is a slow process, but becomes faster at higher temperatures. Hence, on a sunny day, clothes will dry faster.

Explore

Compare the speed of evaporation of water in sunlight and in shade. Take two ceramic plates of the same size. Place one of the plates in sunlight and keep the other in shade. Pour equal amounts of water in each of the plates using a tablespoon or any other measure.

Observe the two plates after every twenty minutes. From which plate does water disappear first? Can you tell the reason?

evaporation: the process of becoming a vapour

The same process happens with sea water on a larger scale. During the day, in the presence of sunlight, the water in the oceans, rivers, lakes and ponds heats up and continuously turns into vapour. In addition, plants on land also give off water vapour through the process of transpiration. The water vapour released from the oceans and plants mixes with air and rises to the sky. As the air containing water vapour moves up, it gets cooler and cooler. At a height of a few thousand metres, the air becomes so cool that the water vapour present in it condenses to form tiny droplets of water. These droplets remain floating in the air and appear as clouds. This process of condensation plays an important role in bringing water back to the surface of the earth.

Water drops in clouds

When the droplets of water in the clouds come together, they form larger-sized drops of water, which become too heavy to remain floating in air and begin to fall as rain. If the temperature of air at that time is very low, the droplets sometimes freeze and fall as hail or snow.

Water falling as rain

Water droplets freeze into snow

Explore

Take a glass half-filled with water. Wipe the glass from the outside with a clean, dry piece of cloth. Put some ice into the water. Wait for a few minutes. Examine the outer surface of the glass again. What do you find?

Can you tell where the water drops on the outer wall of the glass came from? What happens to water vapour when it is cooled?

transpiration: the process of giving off water vapour through the leaves
droplet: a tiny drop
condensation: the process of changing from a gaseous to a liquid or solid state

Most of the water that falls on land as rain and snow sooner or later reaches back into the oceans. Snow falling on the mountains melts into water, which flows down in the form of streams and rivers. Some of the water that falls on land as rain also flows into rivers and streams. Most rivers, after

Snow melting and flowing into the river

covering long distances on land, ultimately flow into seas or oceans, although water from some rivers flow into lakes. Hence, rainwater also fills up lakes and ponds.

River

Explore

Take a large glass or plastic jar with a wide mouth containing salt water. Keep an empty glass at the centre of the jar; such that it is surrounded by salt water. Now cover the mouth of the jar with a transparent polythene sheet and tie it with a string. Take a small piece of stone or any small heavy object and place it in the middle of the plastic sheet such that the plastic sheet forms a depression in the middle just above the empty glass kept inside the jar. Lift the jar carefully and place it in the sun.

Wait till evening. Carefully take off the plastic cover and remove the glass kept inside. Is it still empty? Where did the water come from? Is the water salty? Do you understand now why rainwater is not salty?

Groundwater comes from rain, snow, sleet and hail that seeps into the ground. The water moves down into the ground because of gravity, passing between particles of sand, gravel or rock until it reaches a depth where the ground is saturated or filled with water. This area filled with water is called the **saturated zone** and the top of this zone is called the **water table**.

Factastic

Water is the only substance on earth that exists naturally in three states—solid, liquid and gas.

groundwater: underground water that is held in the soil and in porous rocks

Under certain conditions, rainwater does not get a chance to seep underground. For example, in areas where the land has little or no vegetation, the rainwater flows away quickly without seeping into the ground. Such flowing rainwater also washes away the top layer of the soil with it. In cities where most of the land is covered with concrete or asphalt, there is little seepage of rainwater into the ground. All these factors ultimately reduce the amount of rainwater seeping through the ground and reduces the availability of groundwater.

The sun, which drives the water cycle, heats water in oceans and seas. Water evaporates as water vapour into the air. **Evapotranspiration** is water transpired by plants and evaporated from the soil. Rising air currents take the vapour up to the cooler parts of the atmosphere. Water vapour forms clouds by the process of **condensation** and then

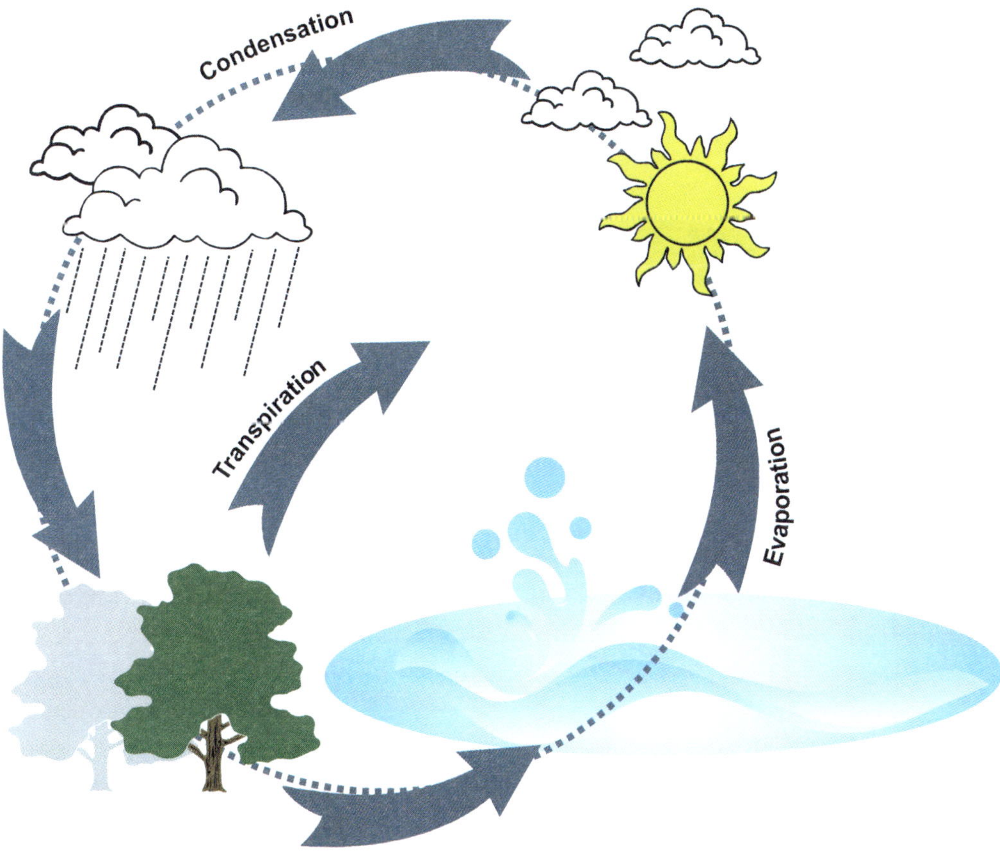

The water cycle

returns to the ground as rain, hail or snow. This water that is brought back to the surface of the earth in the form of rain, hail or snow, finally goes back into the oceans through rivers. The circulation of water in this manner is a continuous process and is known as the **water cycle**. It ensures that the supply of water on land is maintained.

Floods

Rain is an important component of the water cycle, but the amount and duration of rainfall varies widely from place to place. In some parts of the world, it does not rain for years, while there are places where it rains throughout the year. For example, the Atacama Desert in Chile has hardly had any rainfall in the last four centuries, whereas Mawsynram, a small village in the Khasi hills in India, receives about 1,150 centimetres of rain annually, which is the highest in the world.

Flooded village

In India, most of the rainfall occurs during the monsoon season. The sowing of many crops depends on the arrival of monsoon. Optimum rain is important for good food production. Too much or too little of it could be detrimental. When there is little rain, it could dry up the crops. In conditions of excessive rainfall, there is a rise in the level of water in rivers, lakes and ponds, which then spills over the banks and spreads over large areas causing floods. Every year, floods cause havoc in India especially in the flood-prone states. Crops that get submerged in flood waters cannot grow properly and hence are destroyed. Floods also cause loss of human life and destruction of property. Livestock often get carried away during floods. In the aftermath of floods, there is increased risk to humans and animals from various water-borne diseases such as typhoid.

Droughts

Drought

In the absence of a good monsoon season, crops dry up and food production is affected. If it does not rain in a region for a year or more, the soil continues to lose water by evaporation and transpiration, but no water is brought back by rain. In such regions, the soil finally becomes dry and nothing grows in it. The level of water in

flood: the rising of a body of water and its overflowing onto normally dry land

ponds and wells also goes down and some of which may dry up. Groundwater also becomes scarce. All this ultimately leads to a condition known as drought, when it becomes difficult to get water and food for people and fodder for animals. Drought often affects some parts of India and at such times relief measures have to be undertaken by the government to provide food and water to the drought-affected people.

Water tankers

Conserving water

When there is continuous shortage of water, plants, animals and human beings perish and the affected land becomes parched and dry. People who live near or around deserts, where there is limited availability of water, know how precious water is and they take great care using it. They cannot afford to waste water like many of us do.

Parched land

Although the total amount of water on earth remains the same, the water available for use is very limited and is decreasing due to over-usage. Rising population is resulting in the increase in the demand for water. In many cities, long queues for collection of water is now a common sight. Also, more and more water is being used for producing food as well as by the industries. However, despite the rising demands, a large quantity of water can still become available if it is used with care and if wastage is reduced.

drought: a prolonged shortage of rainfall

Factastic
Washing your hands can use up to 14 litres of water while a shower can use 115 to 120 litres.

Rainwater harvesting

India receives plenty of rainwater during the monsoon season every year, but only a small part of it is stored in dams and lakes. Most of it flows back into the oceans through rivers without being used. If rainwater is collected and stored during monsoon to be used later, especially in the summer season, it can greatly increase the amount of water available throughout the year.

There are several methods of collecting and storing rainwater. These are known as **rainwater harvesting** techniques. When rain falls on open fields covered with vegetation, a part of the rainwater seeps underground and is stored as groundwater that can be later drawn by pumps. But rainwater that falls in places that are mostly covered with concrete roads and buildings can only flow into drains and from there to rivers and ultimately to the sea, and thus cannot be used for any practical purpose.

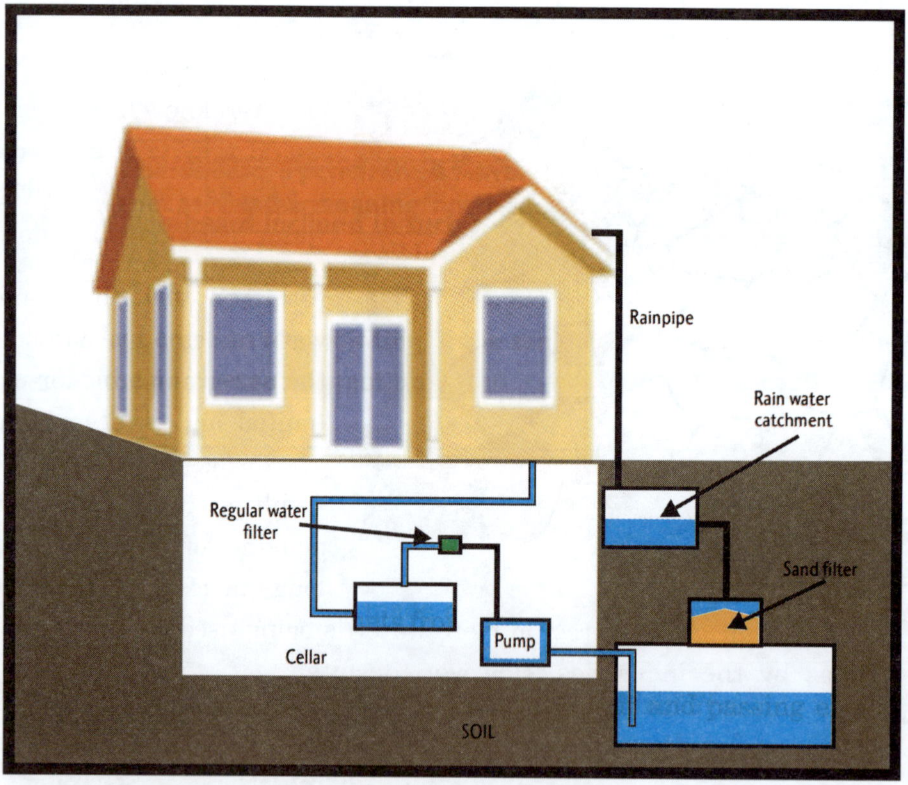

Rooftop rainwater harvesting

The main thought behind rainwater harvesting is to collect the rainwater where it falls. Usually it is passed underground to **recharge** the groundwater so that it can be pumped out and used when needed. In the **rooftop rainwater harvesting** system, the rainwater is collected when it falls on the roofs of houses or buildings and sent to a storage tank, through pipes. The tank may be underground or placed on the ground. This water may contain dirt and leaves that need to be filtered before it is used.

Water stored in tanks cannot last long, hence, water collected from the roof can also be sent through pipes directly into a pit in the ground. This water then seeps into the soil to recharge or refill the groundwater, which can be used for a much longer time.

Rainwater that flows into roadside stormwater drains can also be made to go directly into the ground, for recharging groundwater. Most residential colonies in cities have a proper network of stormwater drains. If maintained neatly, these offer a simple and cost-effective means for harvesting rainwater.

Activity

Aim: To make a coloured fountain.

Material required: **a glass jug or tank filled with cold water, a small glass bottle, hot water and food colour**

Method: **Mix a food colour of your choice in hot water. Fill the glass bottle with the coloured water. Place the bottle into a glass jug or tank filled with cold water and observe.**

Conclusion: **As the warm water rises up, you will be able to see a fountain of coloured water coming out of the bottle and moving up in the tank while the cold water will drift to the bottom.**

Revision Time

* Water is the key to life on earth.
* Water is needed in agriculture for growing food and in industries for producing almost all the things for daily use.
* The water in rivers, lakes and wells is replenished by the waters of the oceans through the process of water cycle.
* The sun heats the water in the seas and oceans. Water evaporates as vapour into the air. Evapotranspiration is water transpired from plants and evaporated from the soil. The water vapour forms clouds due to condensation and that returns to earth as rain, hail, snow or sleet. This cyclic route is called the water cycle.
* Some of the rainwater that falls on land, seeps into the ground, recharging groundwater.
* Rain is an important component of the water cycle, but the amount and duration of rainfall varies widely from place to place.
* Too much rain leads to a rise in the level of water in rivers and lakes causing floods.
* Too little rain causes the soil to become parched and water resources to dry up, leading to droughts.
* If rainwater is collected and stored during monsoon for later use, it could greatly increase the amount of water available throughout the year.

Quiz Time

1. Answer the questions.

a. Where does the tap water in our homes come from?

b. What happens to the snow falling on mountains?

c. How do plants give off water vapour?

d. What happens when there is no rain for a year or more?

e. What is rainwater harvesting?

2. Fill in the blanks.

a. Water makes up almost ____________________ per cent of our body.

b. The source of water in wells is the ____________________.

c. When water is left exposed to air, it ____________ over time.

d. This process of ____________ plays an important role in bringing water back to the surface of the earth.

e. It is ____________ which comes out from a hand pump or a tube well.

3. Indicate whether the statements are true or false.

a.	Water follows a cyclic path in nature.	True	False
b.	Plants on land give off water vapour through the process of condensation.	True	False
c.	The circulation of water between ocean and land is not a continuous process.	True	False
d.	Rainwater harvesting is a method of harvesting crops using rainwater.	True	False
e.	As the air containing water vapour moves up, it gets cooler and cooler.	True	False

4. Explain the terms.

a. drought

b. groundwater

c. groundwater recharge

d. hail

e. water cycle

5. Project Work

Consult reference books in the library and search the internet to find out the different ways of conserving water. Prepare a chart showing the different ways of saving water and preventing water sources from getting polluted. Use photographs cut out from magazines or newspapers, or drawings to illustrate your points.

Think it over

1. Why do floods occur if forests are cut on mountainsides?

2. Why does water obtained from tube wells leave white scales when boiled?

15 All About Air

Air is all around us. It is colourless and odourless and hence we cannot see, smell or feel it unless it moves. We cannot live without air because it contains oxygen, a gas which we breathe in.

When air is not moving, we cannot feel its presence. In summer, a handheld fan creates a cooling effect by moving the air in the surroundings. The pages of an open book begin to flutter when the fan is switched on because of moving air. Paper pinwheels (*chakri*) that children play with spin and kites fly because of moving air. A folded sheet of paper or a piece of stiff card can be used to put out a candle flame by rapidly moving it over the flame several times. The movement of the folded sheet of paper or card creates a blast of air that extinguishes the flame.

Handheld fan

Activity

Aim: To make a paper pinwheel.

Material required: a square piece of paper, a pair of scissors, a pin, a stick and glue

Method: Fold a square piece of paper (about 20 cm x 20 cm) diagonally to make a triangle. Then unfold it and fold it again along the opposite corners. You should now have a pair of folds making an 'X' across the paper.

Mark points about 3 cm from the centre of the 'X' along each of the crease marks with a pencil. Cut a straight line down each crease with a pair of scissors up to the marked points. Grasp one half of the corner you have just cut and pull it down to

oxygen: a colourless, odourless, tasteless, gas that supports burning and constitutes 21 per cent of the earth's atmosphere
pinwheel: a toy consisting of vanes of coloured paper that is pinned to a stick and spins when it is pointed into the wind

the centre of the 'X'. Be careful not to crease it or fold it. Repeat this process with all four corners until they are all in the centre. Use the same side of each cut every time; otherwise the pinwheel will not work. Stick a pin firmly through the centre of the paper, making sure it pokes through all four folded corners, as well as the centre of the paper. The paper should now form a windmill-like pinwheel.

Push the pin with the pinwheel attached through a tall, thin stick. Your pinwheel is ready. Move the pinwheel gently from side to side, blow on it or hold it up to a light breeze to watch it spin. Can you tell why moving air makes the pinwheel spin?

Conclusion: ______________________________

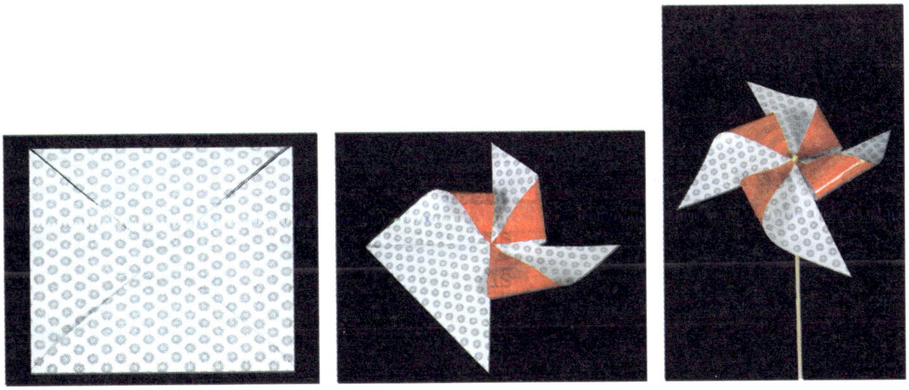

Sailboat and windmill

windmill: a mill or electricity generator that is powered by the wind

Moving air is called wind. Wind can blow gently as a breeze or violently as a storm. Whenever wind blows, it carries with it light materials that fall in its path such as dust, pollens, fallen leaves and pieces of paper and plastic. Blowing wind can be put to many practical uses. For example, the flow of wind is used to separate grains from chaff in fields through a process known as winnowing. Windmills use the energy of the moving air for applications such as grinding grains and generating electricity. Sailboats also use wind energy for moving through water.

Birds, bats, insects, gliders, parachutes and aeroplanes can fly only because there is air. The dispersal of seeds and pollen from flowers of several plants is facilitated by wind. Movement of air plays an important role in the water cycle as well.

Bird, aircraft and kite can fly

However, when wind moves with great speed, it can cause considerable damage. Severe storms can uproot trees and electric poles and rip off thatched and corrugated tin roofs among others.

Air occupies space

We live immersed in an ocean of air, the presence of which is felt only when it moves. We do not realise that air occupies space. But in reality, whichever place on earth looks empty is actually occupied by air. If air is totally removed from any place, a vacuum is created.

Activity

Aim: To observe how air occupies space.

Material requied: a bucket and an empty bottle

Method: Take half a bucket of water. Immerse an empty bottle upside down, with the open mouth at the bottom, into the water. What happens? Does water get into the bottle?

Now, with its mouth still under water, tilt the bottle a little to one side. What happens? What do the bubbles coming out of the bottle contain? Does water get into the bottle now?

From these observations, what do you think was preventing water from getting into the bottle? Was the bottle really empty? What was inside it before water got in?

Conclusion: ______________________________

Air occupies space is a fact that can be confirmed by the following examples. Air is pumped into a football to make it hard and bouncy. Vehicle tyres are filled with air, which act as a very good cushion to support the weight of the vehicle and make the ride comfortable.

Earth's envelope of air

Earth's atmosphere

The air that we breathe is part of an envelope of air that surrounds the earth on all sides. This envelope is known as the atmosphere. The atmosphere extends up to many kilometres above the surface of the earth and gets thinner as one moves away from the ground level. Since air is much thinner on high mountains, it is difficult to breathe there and that is why mountaineers have to carry oxygen cylinders for breathing.

Mountaineers carrying oxygen cylinders

Air is a mixture of different gases.

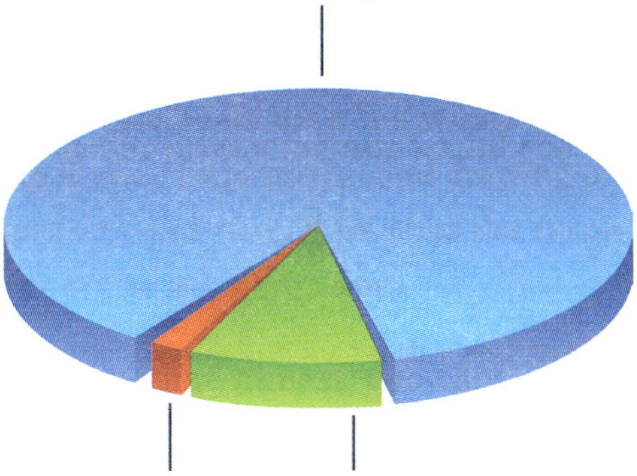

Source of oxygen

The oxygen in air comes mainly from green plants, which make their own food by a process called photosynthesis. During this process, green plants in the presence of chlorophyll take in carbon dioxide from air, water from the soil and use sunlight to manufacture carbohydrates while releasing oxygen into the atmosphere. Plants also consume

atmosphere: the layer of air surrounding the earth

oxygen for respiration, but they produce more of it than they consume. That is why plants are known as the producers of oxygen.

During respiration, animals take in oxygen and give off carbon dioxide, which in turn is used by plants for photosynthesis to produce oxygen. Hence, plants are important for the survival of living things including animals and humans.

Oxygen, nitrogen and carbon dioxide

The oxygen in air not only helps us breathe but also makes it possible for fires to burn. For example, a candle will not burn in the absence of oxygen. In a confined space, a candle will burn only as long as oxygen is available and will go out as soon as the oxygen is used up. A fire can, thus, be extinguished by cutting off the supply of oxygen to the burning material by throwing sand or foam over it.

Nitrogen is a colourless, odourless gas that constitutes seventy-eight per cent of the earth's atmosphere. It does not support combustion.

Explore

When an inverted glass is placed over a burning candle, it continues to burn for a while and then goes off. Till the time there is oxygen, the candle will burn and as soon as the oxygen is consumed, the candle will go off.

Carbon dioxide is a colourless and odourless gas, present in air in very small amounts. It is produced when any carbon-containing material, such as coal, oil, paper or wood, is burnt. Too much carbon dioxide can suffocate and even kill people. In building fires, many people may die, not from burn injuries but due to suffocation by carbon dioxide.

Explore

Take some clear lime water in a flat dish and keep it exposed to air for a day. Do you see a whitish layer on the upper surface of the lime water? Does the lime water turn milky if you stir it? Can you tell what the white layer contains and how it was formed? Does it prove the presence of carbon dioxide in air?

Apart from nitrogen, oxygen and carbon dioxide, air also contains water vapour. But the amount of water vapour in air varies from place to place and from season to season. In desert areas, the amount of water vapour in air is very small whereas near the sea coasts and in tropical forests, the amount of water vapour is high, which makes such areas highly humid. Also, in winter the amount of water vapour present in air is normally low, whereas during summer and the monsoon months it is quite high.

Activity

Aim: To prove that air exerts a lot of pressure.

Material required: a raw potato and a straw

Method: Take a raw potato and place it on a table. Now hold the straw in the middle without covering either ends and try to poke it in the potato. You will notice that the straw can make only small dents in the potato and then bends itself. Now, cover one end of the straw with your thumb and try to poke the other end into the potato. What do you observe?

Observation: The straw is able to poke deep into the potato.

Conclusion: This proves that air has pressure and strength.

Dust and smoke

Sunlight passing through foliage showing dust particles

Air in cities, and even in the countryside, is rarely clean; it contains dust and smoke. That is why even on a clear day, distant objects—buildings, mountains and forests—appear to be hidden behind a haze. Even when the air appears clear, it has lots of dust particles floating in it, which sometimes become visible in bright sunlight. The dust particles make the path of the sunlight that is passing through visible as narrow beams of light.

Explore

monsoon: seasonal winds in southern Asia, bringing rain when blowing from south-west
foliage: a cluster of leaves

Find a room on the sunny side of your home or school that can be made completely dark. If necessary, use black curtains on the doors and windows to make it completely dark. Now open a door just a bit to allow only a thin beam of sunlight to enter the room.

Look at the beam carefully. Do you see something floating in it? What is it? Would you see the floating particles if the air was totally clean?

Smoke from firewood

Smoke is nothing but a cloud of fine particles suspended in air. Smoke is produced when fuel does not burn completely. Smoke is produced during burning of biomass such as firewood, dry leaves, agricultural waste and animal dung cakes in villages and small towns. People in villages burn firewood and animal dung cakes for cooking and heating puposes, polluting the air in the process. Smoke is also produced by industries.

Smoke and dust in air are bad for health. If inhaled, they can cause various respiratory disorders.

Air in water and soil

Human beings and land animals can breathe oxygen directly from the air during respiration. However, fish and some other animals that live in water, get their oxygen from the air dissolved in water. If water gets polluted, the amount of dissolved oxygen becomes less and sometimes fish die in large numbers. Also, air dissolved in water escapes as bubbles if the water is heated because at high temperatures less air can dissolve in water.

Explore

Take water in a container and heat it slowly on a burner. Look at the inner surface of the container after about a minute. What do you see?

pores: tiny holes through which liquids and gases can pass

Air is present in the soil too. About half of the total mass of soil is made up of vast interconnecting pores. These pores are filled

Animal burrows

Earthworms in soil

with both air and water. The amount of air and the amount of water filling these spaces varies dramatically through the year and from location to location. The air found in soil is very different from the air found in the atmosphere since it is not exposed to moving air currents, and hence is much more moist, or humid. It also tends to be rich in carbon dioxide and poor in oxygen.

Many animals, such as moles, rats and snakes, which live underground, use this for respiration. They make burrows and holes that make spaces available for air to move in and out of the soil. But when it rains heavily, water fills up all the spaces occupied by the air in the soil, forcing animals living in the soil to come out to breathe. That is why earthworms and snakes usually come out of the soil during heavy rains.

Revision Time

* Air is all around us but cannot be seen because it has no colour.
* Moving air can be felt.
* Air occupies space.
* The air that we breathe is part of the earth's atmosphere.
* Air is also present in water and soil.
* Air is a mixture of gases such as oxygen, nitrogen, carbon dioxide, water vapour and other trace gases.
* The oxygen in air comes mainly from green plants, which is released during the process of photosynthesis.
* Oxygen supports burning and is necessary for living organisms.
* Carbon dioxide is produced when any carbon-containing material, such as coal, oil, paper or wood, is burnt. Carbon dioxide is present in air in very small amounts.
* Even when the air appears clear, it has lots of dust particles floating in it.
* Animals that live in water use oxygen dissolved in water for respiration.

Quiz Time

1. Answer the questions.

a. What are the main gases present in air?

b. Which gas present in air do plants use for photosynthesis?

c. What is the layer of air that envelops the earth called?

d. Why does a candle go out if covered with a glass?

e. In which season is the amount of water vapour present in air the highest?

2. Fill in the blanks.

a. Fish use oxygen ____________________ in water for respiration.

b. Plants give off oxygen during ____________________.

c. An empty bottle is actually filled with ____________________.

d. A candle flame goes out in the ____________________ of oxygen.

e. Lime water kept exposed to air becomes cloudy because of the presence of ____________________ in air.

3. Indicate whether the statements are true or false.

a.	Air contains 78 per cent oxygen and 21 per cent nitrogen.	True	False
b.	Plants use carbon dioxide from air and water from soil in the presence of sunlight to produce food.	True	False
c.	A fire can be extinguished by cutting off the supply of oxygen to the burning material.	True	False
d	Even when the air appears clear, it has lots of dust particles floating in it.	True	False
e.	The soil does not contain any air.	True	False

4. Explain the terms.

a. atmosphere

b. chlorophyll

c. smoke

d. windmill

e. carbon dioxide

5. Project Work

Observe the leaves of trees, shrubs or bushes planted by the roadside near your house, in a neighbourhood garden and in your school compound. They may have some dust or soot deposited on them. Wipe a few leaves of a few trees or shrubs with a wet piece of cloth. You may choose only leaves that you can reach easily. Carefully mark the trees or shrubs, whose leaves you have cleaned, by tying a ribbon around its trunk/stem.

Go back to the same trees and shrubs after a few days and observe how much dust and soot has collected on the leaves you had cleaned earlier. Is the amounts of dust and soot deposited on the leaves in the three areas the same or are they different? Where do you find the deposits thickest? What could be the possible reasons for this difference? Carry out the same experiment for trees near a factory or power house in your area.

Compare your data with that of your classmates. Mark your combined findings on a map of your city. In this way, you can identify which parts of the city are most polluted and those that have the least amount of pollution.

Think it over

1. **Why does the air get thinner and cooler as you go up on a mountain?**
2. **Why can't an aircraft fly in space?**

16 Dealing with Garbage

Garbage is produced in every household, office, shop, hotel, restaurant, hospital and in places where people live and work. Common garbage includes kitchen waste, packaging material, waste paper, polythene bags, broken plastic toys, old and torn clothes, shoes and slippers. The waste produced by hospitals, poultry farms and abattoirs needs special care in handling and disposal. If garbage is not removed and disposed off properly, it may create serious health problems.

Truck dumping garbage

Ragpickers rummaging through garbage

Most waste produced in cities is thrown into garbage bins. Out of the waste that is generated, there are several things that can be used again. These include metal cans and objects, plastic objects and broken glass objects. The rest of the waste is then carried by municipal trucks to the outskirts of cities and dumped in low-lying areas called landfills and covered with a layer of soil. Once the landfill is completely full, it can be converted into a park. However, since the soil in the landfill area is not

garbage: any matter that is no longer wanted or needed
disposal: the act or means of getting rid of something
landfill: a low area where waste is buried between layers of soil

compact, no building construction is allowed on it for at least twenty years.

Landfill

Activity

Aim: To convert the kitchen waste into compost.

Material required: kitchen waste including fruit and vegetables peels and non-biodegradable materials

Method: Separate the garbage in your house into two groups. In Group 1, put kitchen waste such as fruit and vegetable peels, tea leaves, eggshells, waste food, dry leaves and paper bags. In Group 2, put polythene bags, plastic spoons, Thermocol cups, glass pieces, aluminium wrappers, nails and broken toys.

Dig two pits in the ground. Put the waste from Group 1 into one pit and garbage in Group 2 in the other pit.

After four to five days, remove the soil from the pits and examine the state of the garbage in the pits.

Only when the garbage has a black colour and emits no foul smell would the rotting process be complete. Examine the garbage in the pits again after every two or three days and again after a couple of weeks.

Observation: Record your observations in the blank column.

Rotted completely and no smell	
Rotted partially	
Rotted almost completely, but still smelt bad	
No change at all	
How much time did it take for the waste to rot?	

Garbage usually contains two kinds of wastes—biodegradable wastes and non-biodegradable wastes. Biodegradable wastes can be broken down and decomposed by soil bacteria. It will ultimately rot. Examples are vegetable waste, food waste, leaves, paper, wood, etc. However, non-biodegradable wastes, such as plastics, metal and glass, cannot be decomposed by soil bacteria and will not rot. Biodegradable wastes can be turned into compost and used as a valuable organic fertiliser while non-biodegradable wastes will remain unchanged for many years.

biodegradable: capable of being decomposed by bacteria
decompose: break down into simpler products

Composting garbage

The rotting and conversion of biodegradable materials into organic fertiliser is called 'composting'. To make it easier to separate biodegradable and non-biodegradable waste from garbage before it is sent to landfills, municipalities in some cities and towns provide separate dustbins for collecting the two kinds of garbage. Bins for biodegradable wastes are usually coloured green, while those meant for non-biodegradable wastes are coloured blue. Waste dumped in the green bins can be buried and turned into **compost** while waste dumped in the blue bins that includes plastics, metals and glass, can be recycled. Compost or manure is obtained through a natural process where the nutrients in the waste are recycled.

Factastic

If buried in a landfill, it takes plastic soda bottles and glass a million years; disposable baby diapers, 500 years; aluminium cans fifty to 200 years; batteries 100 years; and paper one to five months to decompose in the soil.

Blue and green bins

In some places, garbage, especially dry leaves, waste paper and tyres are burnt. The smoke and gases thus produced pollute the air and are harmful for health. Rather than burning, dry leaves can be turned into compost. Agricultural waste, such as straw and husk, can be used for growing mushrooms and for various other purposes.

Burning dry leaves

Vermicomposting

vermicomposting: a technique of using earthworms to turn organic wastes into very high quality compost

The process of composting can be speeded up by using earthworms, which naturally live underground. The process is called vermicomposting. In the process, earthworms eat and digest kitchen and farm wastes and turn out high quality compost or manure. A special

Red worms for vermicomposting

type of earthworm called **red worm** is used in vermicomposting. India is one of the leading countries where vermicomposting is widely applied by thousands of small farmers and many industries to produce organic fertiliser.

Vermicomposting is quite simple. It can be done in a pit about 30-cm deep or in a wooden box kept in a place, which is neither too hot, nor too cold since red worms do not survive in extreme temperature conditions. They also need moisture around them hence the pit or the wooden box should be away from direct sunlight. The procedure involves spreading a net or chicken mesh at the bottom of the pit or the box or, in the alternative, layering it with an 1-2-cm thick layer of sand. After that, vegetable wastes including peels of fruits and vegetables, green leaves, pieces of newspaper and dried dung, are spread over the wire mesh or layer of sand. Water is sprinkled in moderation to make this layer wet. The wet layer of waste is not pressed but kept loose so that it contains sufficient air and moisture.

Factastic

In a day a red worm can eat food equal to its own weight.

After the pit is ready, red worms can be bought from the market and put in it. The pit is then covered loosely with an old sheet of cloth, a gunny bag or a layer of grass. The top layers of the pit need to be gently turned and moved once every few days.

If proper care is taken, the number of red worms in the pit will double in a month's time. It takes about four weeks for the vermicompost to be ready, which is indicated when the waste put in the pit turns into a loose, soil-like material.

Factastic

Red worms do not have teeth, but have a structure called gizzard, which helps them in grinding their food. The presence of powdered eggshells or seashells can help red worms in grinding their food.

gizzard: thick-walled muscular pouch used for grinding food

At this stage, if some vegetable wastes are placed as food in one corner of the pit, most of the worms will shift towards that part of the pit. The compost can then be removed from the vacated part and dried in the sun for a few hours to make it ready for use. The vermicompost thus produced is a valuable organic fertiliser that can be used in pots, gardens or fields. The worms remaining in the pit can be used for preparing more compost or can be shared with another user.

Making of vermicompost from waste is a good example of turning waste into wealth since expensive chemical fertilisers need not be purchased. Besides reducing the application of chemical fertilisers that is harmful to the environment, the use of vermicompost also reduces the water requirement of the plants because of its moisture-holding capacity.

The quantity of garbage

The amount of garbage produced by a family depends essentially on their lifestyle. If a family uses a lot of packaged items of food, groceries, milk and bottled water, the amount of packaging material thrown away per day would be considerable. But if a family buys loose items of food, groceries and milk, the amount of garbage produced would be much less. The judicious use of disposable items, such as paper plates, plastic cups, plastic spoons, especially in weddings and birthday parties, and items that come in individual packaging can go a long way in reducing the amount of garbage produced.

Paper, jute and cloth bag

Besides, many discarded items that are normally thrown away can be used in innovative ways. Pen and pencil holders from soft drink cans, greeting cards decorated with dried flowers or flowers made from pencil shavings, mats from old clothes, papier-mâché items from newspaper waste, toys

disposable: designed to be thrown out after use

from discarded rubber soles of sandals and drinking straws, and baskets from used old polythene bags are some items that can be made from waste materials.

Factastic

On an average, every person in the United States produces 1.8 kg of waste, in Australia 1.6 kg, in Japan 0.6 kg, and in India 0.4 kg each day. More than one-third of the waste generated can be recycled.

Recycling

Recycling is the process of collecting materials that are often considered waste

Conservation tips

Given is a list of activites that help in conservation. Tick mark the ones that you already practice at home and put a star on the activities that you will now intitiate.

1. Donate old toys and clothes to charity instead of throwing them away. ☐
2. Use both sides of a blank paper instead of only one side for writing or photocopying. ☐
3. Use a bucket instead of a shower to conserve water. ☐
4. Do not leave the tap on while brushing your teeth. ☐
5. Use reusable shopping bags made of paper or cloth. ☐
6. Use reusable snack or lunch boxes instead of disposable ones. ☐
7. Initiate car pools for school or other after school activities. A reduced number of cars on the road will reduce fuel consumption and also emit less exhaust. ☐
8. Turn off the lights when you leave a room and also unplug electric toys and gadgets when not in use. ☐
9. Recycle as many things as you can including magazines, newspapers, metal cans, glass bottles and plastic containers. ☐
10. Use rechargeable batteries instead of disposable ones. ☐

and using them to manufacture new products that can be used again. Many things of daily use can be recycled. They include, clear glass bottles and jars, plastic bottles, shampoo and motor oil containers, aluminium cans, newspaper, magazines and coloured paper to name a few. Components of several products, such as computers, are recyclable. Automobile tyres can be broken down and reused for making road surfaces.

Brainteaser

Recycling is a process by which we can reuse waste items. Give one practical way in which you can reuse the following kitchen items.

1. leftover vegetables
2. leftover cooked rice
3. empty cheese tin
4. empty cola bottles
5. empty cardboard cartons
6. empty cold drink cans
7. empty oil cans
8. old dusters, cloth or board
9. empty ice cream cups
10. chipped utensils

Explore

Aim: To make hand-made paper.

Material required: old paper to be recycled, a wire mesh, a tub and a kitchen roller

Method: Collect old newspapers, used envelopes, notebooks or waste paper from the school office. Get the carpenter to make a wooden frame fitted with a wire mesh.

Tear the paper into small pieces and soak them in water in a tub or a bucket for a day. Take out the wet pieces of paper and pound them with a mallet to make a pulp. Spread the wet pulp evenly on the wire mesh fixed to the frame and wait till water drains off. Spread a few sheets of newspaper on the pulp layer to soak up more water.

Carefully lift the layer of pulp from the frame, place it between a few sheets of newspaper and run a kitchen roller (*belan*) over it to squeeze out as much water as possible. Now, place the pulp

sheet on a few dry sheets of newspaper and keep it in the sun to dry. When it becomes completely dry, you will have hand-made paper. If you add colour, pieces of dried grass or leaves, flower petals or pieces of coloured paper in the pulp before spreading, it will produce beautiful patterns on the hand-made paper. By this process you can make hand-made paper of many shades and designs, which can also be used to make beautiful greeting cards.

Recycling has several benefits.

- It helps conserve natural resources such as wood, water and minerals.
- It saves energy because lesser quantity of new products will need to be manufactured.
- Recycling indirectly reduces the production of greenhouse gases because industries burn less fossil fuel.
- It also prevents the destruction of natural habitats and reduces soil erosion associated with mining and logging.

Plastic and associated problems

Plastic is a versatile and potentially indestructible material, which makes it ideal for a number of commercial and household uses. We use many plastic objects in our daily life, such as toothbrushes, toothpaste tubes, combs, plastic buckets, mugs and shoes with polyurethane soles, to name a few. Indeed, it may be a little difficult to imagine our life without plastics today. Plastic has replaced material such as glass, porcelain, brass, steel, wood, jute and many others. Most plastic items of daily use, such as bottles, bags, plates, glasses, spoons and packaging of all kinds, are disposable. They are meant to be thrown away after use. The known fact is that plastic is non-biodegradable. Some plastic can be recycled, but collecting them and processing them is quite expensive. Hence, not much plastic that is thrown away is recycled and this has become a big environmental concern today.

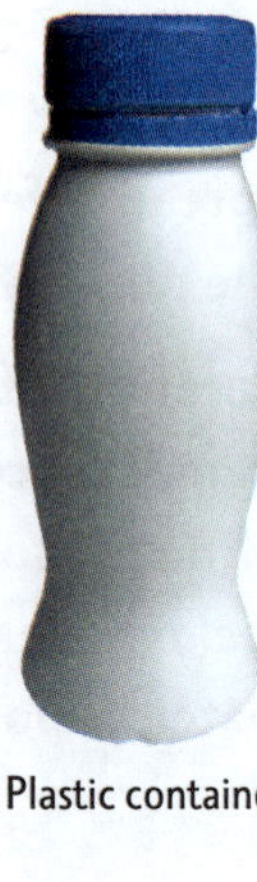
Plastic container

The indiscriminate use and disposal of plastic bags has become a problem. Carelessly thrown away plastic bags are known to choke drains creating flood-like situations in heavy rain. Cattle are known to have died while trying to eat vegetable waste-filled plastic bags. A large proportion of plastic winds up in the ocean, where it is often torn into small particles which are eaten by marine animals. This causes a possible serious threat to the food chain, as the marine animals are eaten by other animals. Despite a ban on plastic bags, rampant use continues in our country, although a few state governments have succeeded in enforcing the ban strictly.

Ways to reduce waste

The point to remember is that plastic may not be harmful if used with care and in such a way that it poses no threat to the environment.

- Use cotton or jute bags for shopping rather than plastic bags.
- Used plastic bags should never be thrown away randomly.
- Create awareness among people about the need to reduce consumption, and reuse and recycle as much as possible rather than throwing things away.
- Glass bottles are better for milk packaging and soft drinks rather than plastic pouches and bottles because glass bottles can be washed and reused
- Vermicomposting should be practised to tackle the problem of disposal of kitchen and farm waste at home, especially in small towns and villages.
- The three important words begining with R are: **Reduce** the use of non-biodegradable items; **Reuse** whenever possible to reduce waste generation; **Recycle** items so that less waste is generated.

Revision Time

- ✶ Garbage is produced in every household, office, shop, hotel, restaurant, hospital and in places where people live and work.
- ✶ Most waste produced in cities is carried by municipal trucks to the outskirts of cities and dumped and then buried in low-lying areas called landfills.
- ✶ Garbage usually contains two kinds of wastes–biodegradable and non-biodegradable.
- ✶ Biodegradable waste can be broken down and decomposed by soil bacteria and will ultimately rot, but non-biodegradable waste cannot be decomposed by soil bacteria and will not rot.
- ✶ The rotting and conversion of biodegradable materials into organic fertiliser is called composting.
- ✶ In vermicomposting, earthworms are used to produce high quality compost in less time.
- ✶ The amount of garbage produced by a family depends a lot on their lifestyle.
- ✶ The limited use of disposable items can go a long way in reducing the amount of garbage produced.
- ✶ Recycling is the process of collecting materials that are often considered waste and using them to manufacture new products that can be resold and used again.
- ✶ One of biggest problems today is the indiscriminate use and disposal of plastic bags, which often choke drains and kill animals.
- ✶ The problem of garbage disposal can be tackled to a large extent by creating awareness among people about the need to reduce consumption, and reuse and recycle as much as possible.

Quiz Time

1. Answer the questions.

a. What are landfills?

b. Which is a better option for serving food in a party—plastic plates or banana leaves. Why?

c. What are biodegradable wastes?

d. Why is using vermicompost better than using chemical fertilisers?

e. Why are glass bottles better for selling soft drinks than plastic bottles?

2. Fill in the blanks.

a. Vegetable waste, food waste, leaves, paper, wood, etc., are all ____________ wastes.

b. The rotting and conversion of vegetable materials into organic fertiliser is called ____________.

c. Garbage bins for biodegradable waste are usually coloured ____________.

d. Red worms do not have teeth but have a structure called ____________, which helps them in grinding their food.

e. ____________ is the process of collecting materials that are often considered waste and using them to manufacture new products that can be resold and used again.

3. Indicate whether the statements are true or false.

a.	Once a landfill is completely full, buildings can be constructed on it.	True	False
b.	Biodegradable waste can be turned into compost and used as a valuable organic fertiliser.	True	False
c.	Garbage bins meant for non-biodegradable waste are coloured green.	True	False
d.	Vermicomposting uses earthworms to eat and digest kitchen wastes and turn out high quality compost.	True	False
e.	Recycling saves energy because less energy is used to manufacture brand new products.	True	False

4. Explain the terms.

a. landfill

b. biodgradable

c. compost

d. vermicomposting

e. recycle

5. Project Work

From the activities described in this chapter, you may have some idea about biodegradable and non-biodegradable objects. Look at the objects around you and put their names in the first column in as shown in the table given below. List as many objects as possible. In the second column, against each of them, write down whether it is biodegradable or non-biodegradable.

Object	Biodegradable/Non-biodegradable
wooden table	biodegradable
plastic chair	non-biodegradable
flower	
potato peel	
porcelain dinner plate	
leather shoes	
straw hat	
cotton shirt	
foam cushion	
banana	

Think it over

1. **Why is it not advisable to feed red worms used in vermicomposting with wastes that may contain salt, pickles, oil, vinegar, meat and milk preparations?**
2. **Why should plastic wastes never be disposed off by burning?**

Evaluation Sheet

Name: ____________________________

Date: ______________________

Skills	Remarks
Work habits	
Observation skills	
Recollection of scientific terms, facts and definitions	
Understanding and co-relation of concepts and processes	
Application and integration of different concepts	
Diagrammatic skills	
Acquisition of required skills	
Representation or explaining processes or observed phenomena	
Numerical ability	
Analysis of information	